Human stress, work and job satisfaction

OCCUPATIONAL SAFETY
AND HEALTH SERIES
No. 50

HUMAN STRESS,
WORK AND JOB SATISFACTION

A CRITICAL APPROACH

T. M. Fraser

INTERNATIONAL LABOUR OFFICE GENEVA

ISBN 92-2-103042-3
ISSN 0078-3129

First published 1983
Second impression 1984

Printed by the International Labour Office, Geneva, Switzerland

PREFACE

This study is concerned with man in his working environment, and as such involves the disciplines of physiology, psychology, sociology, ergonomics, clinical medicine and systems engineering. No one person can be a specialist in all these fields. In consequence, this paper is not written for the specialist; it is written by and for the generalist, who has a little knowledge in all these areas, and perhaps specialist knowledge in some, but wishes to see as best he can the totality of the inter-relationships occurring amongst the tangibles and intangibles of work, job satisfaction and stress. The specialist can seek more refined data in his specialist literature.

Prof. T.M. Fraser,
Director,
Centre for Occupational Health and Safety,
University of Waterloo, Ontario.

TABLE OF CONTENTS

THE PROBLEM

1

There is a widespread belief amongst those concerned with
influencing the social consciousness of the more advanced
industrial societies that despite the amelioration of physical
working conditions, hailed over the last half century and more,
the ambiance of work is becoming increasingly less tolerable in
most levels of working society.   The days of exploitation in an
inhumane environment may be to some extent gone, but the dangers and
the indignities residing therein have been replaced, at least in
part, by other more subtle and intangible threats.

The substance of this belief is predicated on recognition of
the fact that while the requirements for the workforce have changed
with both industrialisation and the development of technology, and
while the character of the workforce has also changed as its members
have progressively become more educated, more skilled and more
productive, the change in demand for work skills has not developed
in parallel with the change in character of the workforce.   Thus
it is argued that a considerable proportion of workers at all levels
may be called upon to perform depersonalised or perhaps inherently
stressful tasks in an alien, restrictive, and socially pressured
environment, with resulting personal dissatisfaction or even sickness,
social unrest and economic disruption.

If in fact this is so, and there is some justification for the
belief, how has it come about?   As noted, there would appear to be
two elements: a change in the industrial requirements for skills
and a change in the attitudes and aspirations of workers.   As far
as skill requirements are concerned, four factors may be observed.

Firstly, with the development of technology and the assumption by machines and semi-automated processes of much of the work that was previously done by man, there is a greatly reduced need for the practice in industry of the creative arts and the manual crafts. These, by their very nature, demanded dedication and personal involvement, but they returned a dividend in the satisfaction of achievement. Secondly, even the requirements for physical strength and manual dexterity, of which a man might be proud, are disappearing from contemporary industry as machine power replaces human power.

Thirdly, technology has created a new demand among relatively low-level workers for repetitive skills involving neuromuscular co-ordination, vigilance, minor decision making under externally paced conditions, along with a need for the emotional resources required to cope with the social pressures encountered. The combination of skills and resources so required is one found in few persons but demanded of many. Fourthly, the hierarchical system which has been developed for management of industry has demanded a new category of supervisory worker with an intellectual and executive capacity beyond the reach of a good proportion of the workforce.

These four factors, and no doubt others, have contributed towards a change in attitude about work among the workers, and particularly the younger workers, that has developed over the years. In addition, in developed countries in particular, the prosperity that has resulted from the application of technology and the resulting raised educational and cultural level of the workers, has changed their aspirations with respect to the work they seek, as well as to the conditions in which it is performed and the reward they expect to attain. With a reduced opportunity for personal involvement, there is at the same time, and no doubt in compensation, an increased demand for safe, healthy, and comfortable conditions, increased participation in organisation and planning of work, and in decisions affecting their persons, and more human relationships with supervisors and management. Paramount, however, and perhaps a motivating force for demand, is a feeling of increased insecurity induced by the existence of vague threatening factors, social, managerial, and environmental, that may have personal impact but are outside personal control.

Technology and industrialisation have also brought about another change, significant in this regard, namely a change in the nature of stress itself.

To primitive man, perhaps right up to the beginnings of the Industrial Revolution, stress was most probably a readily definable, clearly identifiable state, often urgent and life-threatening but, in a sense, tangible. Man responded to stress by the action that his physiology and behavioural patterns demanded of him, and in so doing purged himself of the stress-induced demands. He may have lived at a survival level in recurrent fear, but it is doubtful if he suffered from psychosomatic disease induced by work. Contemporary man is still exposed to stress, and while at times it may be life-threatening and amenable only to fight or flight (to use Cannon's term), more often it is relatively less intensive, not susceptible to personal corrective action, and leaves him strained and tense, ready for battle but unable to define the real enemy.

To anyone knowledgeable in the field, the foregoing views are already appreciated, if not definitively outlined. Intuitively, one can perceive an inter-relationship among work, stress and job satisfaction. Since many of the factors involved are intangible, and some are not defined in any respect, it is difficult, however, to establish the nature and effect of this inter-relationship. It is to this problem then that this study addresses itself, namely the need to define and delineate the factors involved, to establish the inter-relationship, and to determine its effects.

The basic factors, work, stress, and job satisfaction, are vast in their scope, intangible to a greater or less degree in their definition, and transdisciplinary in the knowledge requirements of their fields. Any attempt to embrace the totality of the problem from the viewpoint of a specialist, be he psychologist, sociologist, or physiologist, must therefore be doomed to failure. What is required instead is the viewpoint of the generalist who can attempt to place in perspective the components of the total picture. To do so he may turn to the approach that has been developed in systems engineering, and consider man as an interactive component of, and working within, a functioning system.

In this regard, Carpentier (1974) has stated: "In the determinist models of the last century each factor formed a link in a well defined chain of cause and effect; they postulated limited, closed and programmable systems which provided a logical basis for specialisation and the division of work. In present day models, which deal with live factors, each element is regarded as the consequence of a wider range of relationships and interactions in systems that are open to external influences: the resulting over-all trends are often unpredictable and random; the notion of specialisation is replaced by concepts of totality and adjustment which are necessary for the survival and optimisation of the whole."

In a related frame of reference, looking not strictly at work, but at population, environment, and the quality of life, Levi and Anderson (1974) state: "What may be good from one point of view (say, economy) may be bad from another (say, health) and vice versa. Correspondingly, what may be good for one component in th ecosystem (e.g. economic growth due to rapid industrialisation) can be bad for another ... Accordingly, the only rational approach is to integrate all specialised strategies, taking into account the entire ecosystem, and continuously evaluating the outcome not just in economic terms, or technological, or in terms of physical, or mental, or social well-being, but concomitantly in all these measures."

Now it may not be feasible to do all that Levi and Anderson suggest, but the approach of systems-thinking does provide a frame of reference in which to work.

THE GLOBAL PERSPECTIVE:
MAN AS A SYSTEM AND A SYSTEM COMPONENT

2

A system is defined as a set of interactive components operating together to perform a function. Each component of a system may itself be a system with its own components, and each subcomponent may be still further subdivided at whatever arbitrary levels one chooses. Each system has an equilibrium state and a function. The equilibrium state is determined by the interactions that occur among the components; and the effectiveness of the function is influenced by the stability of the equilibrium. The fact that the components of a system are dynamic and mutually inter-active determines the corollary that no component should be con-sidered in isolation from the system in which it exists, since as soon as the component is isolated both the system and the component change. Such an ideal unfortunately is not always possible to implement, and all too often piecewise analysis of one sort or another is necessary.

Man, of necessity, is a component of many systems. He himself can be regarded as a system, composed of many systems and subsystems, a concept which was established in anatomy, physiology and medicine long before it was ever applied elsewhere. Consideration of man as a component of a system, however, is a relatively new concept forced upon designers, engineers and planners by a developing technology which failed to recognise not only man's limitations and liabilities as part of a joint operation in a technological environment, but also his attributes and assets.

How then did this new concept arise? As technology advanced and as the pace of production, transportation and communication quickened, man was called upon to perform more and more demanding tasks under adverse and time-pressured conditions. Engineers and

physical scientists, little concerned with the limitations and
capacities of man for whose benefit they were ultimately working,
continued development of their technological world in the somewhat
naive belief that if something were humanly possible, then it was
acceptable.   By the beginning of the Second World War, in aviation
in particular, the performance capability of military aircraft was
beginning to outstrip the human capacity for control, with the
inevitable result that the system failed, bringing injury or death
to the operator and damage or destruction to property.

Consideration of the causes underlying this type of situation,
by Sir Edward Bartlett of Cambridge and others, led to the initial
realisation of a concept which today may seem commonplace and self-
evident, namely that man and the machines and devices that he
operates, or is associated with, cannot be considered as independent
entities.   One cannot design and manufacture a machine or device
for human use, be it a hoe, a milling machine or an aircraft, without considering the limitations and capacities of those who are
going to operate or maintain it, or are in other ways going to be
affected by it.   And so the concept of the man-machine system was
born - a man-machine system being defined as an aggregate of men and
machines (or man and machine) operating as a unit to perform a
function.   Thus a worker on a shop floor may not only be part of a
larger system embracing a complete operation; he may also be the
human component of a single-man, single-tool system.

However, a man-machine system, regardless of its nature,
exists within an environment.   And just as one cannot reasonably
consider that man and machine are independent entities, one cannot
consider the man-machine system as being independent of the environment in which it operates.   One then must think in terms of an
interactive man-machine-environment complex in which the components
are in dynamic equilibrium.   Man, machine, and environment
interact with each other.   Man exists within the environment and
interacts with it; he forms an artifact, device, machine, or technology; his activities and requirements define and modify the
machine; the machine, in turn, modifies or determines his activities; man and machine form a system which interacts with the
environment, as does the machine itself, changing the nature of the
environment and, in turn, becoming part of it, while the environment conditions the nature of the machine.

To examine the inter-relationships of work, stress, and job
satisfaction then, one must place them within the context of a man-
machine-environment complex or system.

The man-machine-environment system

There are various ways in which one might make a presentation
or a model of a man-machine-environment system, each no doubt valid.
The schematic model presented as figure 1 is simple and pertinent
but, although attempts have been made to make it comprehensive, no
claim is made that it is either the only or the most complete way
of representing a complex system.   It is modified from a model
originally developed by the author in other ergonomic contexts
(Fraser, 1964;   Fraser, 1975).

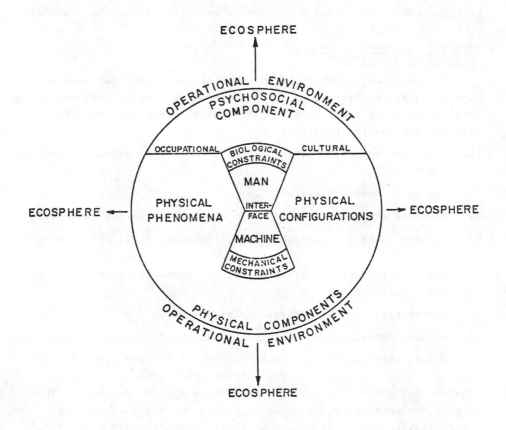

Figure 1:   The man-machine-environment system

As will be seen from the diagram, a man-machine system exists within the environment. Linking man and machine is the all-important interface where there is provision for exchange of information and action between man and machine in the form of displays and controls. The man-machine system cannot, however, interact with the totality of the environment, so that in effect each man-machine system carves out of the ecosphere its own operational environment, specific to that particular system. Since there is in effect an infinite set of man-machine systems, there is also an infinite set of overlapping operational environments. Thus an operational environment might pertain to a man-tool relationship, a man-vehicle relationship, an industry-plant relationship, etc. Operational environments have certain common characteristics which are of significance from the point of view of their effect on man. These can be considered in two main classes, namely the physical component and the psychosocial component.

Physical component of the
operational environment

The physical component of the operational environment can be considered as resulting from an interaction of various phenomena with various states or conditions. The physical phenomena that are involved include the following:

1. force and motion: acceleration, deceleration, vibration, noise, blast, etc.;

2. thermal: heat, cold, humidity;

3. chemical and particulate: toxic chemicals, noxious materials;

4. radiant energy: ionising and non-ionising, e.g., alpha, beta, gamma, X-ray, electron, neutron and other emissions; visible and ultra-violet light; electric and magnetic fields; micro-wave, radio, etc.;

5. barometric: hypo- and hyperbarism, hypoxia;

6. meteorological: i.e., climate and weather.

These phenomena interact with various static and dynamic physical states, conditions, and habitats to produce the proximal physical environment in which a man-machine system operates. Thus certain combinations would occur to define the physical working environment of the industrial shop floor; others would occur for the physical environment of a coal mine or an aircraft.

Psychosocial component of the
operational environment

The psychosocial environment is unique to the human portion of
the system, but since the components of the system are interactive,
the entire system is affected by it.   Levi (1972) defines psychosocial stimuli as those which originate in social relations or
arrangements in the environment which affect the organism through
the mediation of higher nervous processes, and may be suspected under
certain circumstances and in certain individuals of causing disease.
In the model under consideration, the psychosocial component of the
environment includes two elements, namely occupational and cultural.

Occupational: the occupational subcomponent is considered to
include the following:

1.   working hours, shifts, rest periods;

2.   work demands, work procedures, skill demands;

3.   risk and safety status;

4.   supervisory, managerial and workmate relationships.

Again, these factors may interact in various ways to provide
widely varying psychosocial environmental conditions.   In addition,
there are other factors outside of the immediate work environment
which may either condition the general response of the worker to
work, or influence his attitude to the work situation at hand.
These might be termed the cultural subcomponent.

Cultural: the cultural subcomponent can be considered to
include the following:

1.   ethnic background;

2.   urban/rural/migrant habitat;

3.   lifestyle;

4.   peer and domestic relationships.

While the various components and subcomponents of the operational environment have here been analysed and defined somewhat
artificially, and isolated for the purposes of delineation, it is
emphasised that the operational environment is a dynamic whole
within which the man-machine system operates and with some or all
of which it interacts.   Man and machine, of course, have very
different constraints that determine the extent and nature of the
interaction with each other and with the environment.   These can
be outlined as follows:

Human constraints

Human constraints exist within the system since man, of course, is a living being with biological limitations which are relatively insusceptible to modification.   These constraints can be classified as:

(i)   physiological: limitations in power, strength, endurance, and the capacity to maintain homeostasis under adverse conditions, etc.;

(ii) psychological: limitation in learning capacity, skills performance capability, tolerance of adverse conditions and motivation, etc.;

(iii) anthropometric: limitation in morphology, tissue struc- ture, size and shape of work envelope and postural requirements, etc.;

(iv) nutritional: limitations occasioned by need for mainten- ance of appropriate food and water intake and requirements for elimination;

(v)   clinical: limitations occasioned by state of health, pre- sence of disease, accompaniments of ageing, etc.

These various factors combine in diverse ways to affect the nature of the human response and modify the effective system.

Mechanical constraints

Just as there are constraints that affect the human portion of the man-machine system, there are also factors that constrain the mechanical component.   These, in a sense, are analogous to the human constraints with, however, one major difference.   Whereas human constraints are inherent, inescapable, and not always significantly susceptible to modification in the individual, the mechanical constraints exist in the system because they were placed there wittingly or unwittingly by the system designer and are open to modification.   They can be classified as constraints arising out of:

(i)   unsuitability of design: a machine or device can do only what it is designed to do.   If the design is inadequate the function will be imperfect; -

(ii)   unsuitability of materials: the materials selected for
       the structure may be inappropriate to the purpose;

(iii) unsuitability of construction: despite adequacy of
       design and choice of materials the construction may be
       unsatisfactory.

If any, or some combination, of these is at fault the effectiveness of the system will be compromised. This compromise may be
manifest in function, in effect on the man or on the environment, or
in any combiantion of these.

System overload

The system functions in a dynamic equilibrium. Within a range
of tolerances, determined by the components and their limitations,
some acceptable variation from the optimum is permissible. When the
balance is disturbed beyond the permissible limits (which may vary
from time to time and circumstance to circumstance) an overload or
stress will exist. The source of the overload normally lies in the
physical or psychosocial environment, or at the man-machine interface. Ultimately, since it is an interactive system, the effect of
that stress will show itself as a strain somewhere in the system.
Since the machine portion of the system can be designed to meet all
foreseeable strain then the most significant effects from an
anthropocentric viewpoint will be manifest in the weakest component
of the system, namely the man himself.

The nature of this human strain and the psychophysiological
mechanism involved in its occurrence are examined in the next
chapter.

THE PSYCHOPHYSIOLOGY OF HUMAN STRESS

3

Because of its connotations and the diversity of its usage, stress has always been a difficult term to define.   To some, stress describes the state of a physical body which has been sub-jected to pressures or forces close to or beyond its tolerance; to others the term describes the phenomena which produce these pressures or forces.   To some , stress is a physical entity associated with physical change;   to others stress is subjective and associated with psychological and emotional conditions.   To some, stress and strain are synonymous;   to others they are descriptive of cause and effect.

However, regardless of whether one refers to the condition in man as stress or strain, there is a tendency among many to consider it as a <u>pathological</u> human response to psychological, social, occupational and/or environmental pressures.   This, however, is not so.   Hans Selye, the founder of stress physiology, has stated (Selye, 1974):   "Contrary to widespread belief, stress is not simply nervous tension nor the result of damage.   Above all, stress is not necessarily something to be avoided.   It is associated with the expression of all our innate drives.   Stress ensues as long as a demand is made in any part of the body.   Indeed, complete freedom from stress is death!"   Consistent with this viewpoint, although perhaps inconsistent in terminology, the International Symposium on Society, Stress and Disease, sponsored by the World Health Organisation and the University of Uppsala at Stockholm, 1972, adopted as a definition the statement that: "Stress is the non-specific response of the organism to any demand made of it", thus placing themselves squarely in the camp that considers that stress is the response and not the causative state.

While perhaps the point is academic, pursuit of which may
lead to fruitless semantic discussion, the viewpoint that stress
is the resulting and not the causative state is in direct opposition
to the views of the physical scientists and engineers who originally
defined the term.   In fact, even Selye himself has publicly stated
(Harry G. Armstrong Lecture of the Aerospace Medical Association,
1972) that where he originally used the term stress he should have
used strain.   Perhaps, however, the term in its above-defined
meaning is now too well established in psychophysiology and
psychosomatic medicine to be changed.   In physical terms, however,
stress exists when a force is applied to distort a body.   The
effect is manifest as elastic or non-elastic distortion and is
measurable as strain.   The relationship between stress and strain
can be plotted in the form of a curve, which demonstrates that,
with the initial application of stress to an elastic object, some
unmeasurable change will occur in the object, probably not recti-
linear in its relationship to the causative stress.   As the stress
continues there is a measurable strain directly proportional to the
stress.   This is the region of elastic distortion, and if the
stress applied to this level is removed then the strain will also
disappear.   In other words, at this level conditions are reversible.   There is some point, however, at which the stress is such
that there is no longer a direct proportional relationship between
stress and strain.   The stressed object changes its character and
the resulting strain is not reversible.   An elastic band, for
example, will stretch beyond recovery.

There is a psychophysiological analogue of this stress/strain
relationship.   The initial portion of the curve represents a non-
measurable, perhaps cellular or biochemical, response to the
mildest of human stress.   As the stress increases, various physiological and psychological changes can be observed proportional to
the stress, and significantly, reversible when the stress is removed.
With still further increase in stress we enter the realm of pathology, beyond the level of adaptation, where the changes are not
reversible, and some trauma, mental/or physical, results.

By this analogy, stress describes the stimulus state, and strain
the response, although the difference is more one of usage than
meaning.

Homeostasis and feedback control

Regardless of the semantics involved, to examine the psycho-physiological mechanisms of human stress it is necessary first to examine the mechanisms responsible for control of the human organism in the relatively unstressed state.

As noted earlier, man is a complex of systems and subsystems. Co-ordinated control is exerted over this complex to maintain it in the state of dynamic equilibrium to which of course is given the term homeostasis. The purpose of human physiological function is to maintain homeostasis, or more specifically, to maintain the internal environment of the body in a state of chemical and thermal stability in the face of constant change, or threat of change.

Some of this control is inherent in the individual cell, which is itself a complex system, the functions of which can be modified by specialised chemicals, or hormones, secreted by glands of the endocrine system. Over-all control and co-ordination of the entire system is exerted via the central nervous system, through the network of the autonomic nervous system.

The principles of control are the same as for any other system of interactive variables. Pre-set standards are established at levels within which a variable may function. The resulting function is monitored by a sensory mechanism which transmits or feeds back information to co-ordinating centres in the brain. In the centres incoming information is compared with the pre-set standard. If significant variation is found, instructions are issued via the nervous system and glands to effect appropriate change in function. There is thus a closed-loop operation with an input, some means of processing, and an output, which in turn affects the input. The loop and other interacting loops are activated to reach and maintain equilibrium. Thus, there are acceptable limits within which body function may be permitted to vary. Stress, however, provides the stimulus for change in those limits, or, in other words, for adaptation.

General Adaptation Syndrome

Based on work begun in the 1930s, and continued through to this date, Hans Selye in 1950 published a comprehensive theory of

the human response to stress which he termed the General Adaptation
Syndrome.   To put it briefly, he states that there are three
definable stages to the human stress response, namely the stage of
alarm, the stage of resistance and the stage of exhaustion.

The alarm stage occurs as a reaction to a perceived threat and
is characterised by pallor, sweating, increased heart rate,
redistribution of blood to the muscles, etc. It has been described
as preparing the body for "fight or flight".   It is normally short
in duration (a few seconds to a few days) and if the stress persists,
it is replaced by the stage of resistance.   This resistance is a
resistance to those factors which constitute the stress.   During
the stage of resistance most of the signs and symptoms associated
with the alarm reaction disappear as the body develops an adaptation
to the stressful condition.   The capacity to resist, however, is
limited, and should the stress be sufficiently severe or endure
sufficiently long, the stage of resistance will be replaced by a
stage of exhaustion characterised by some form of failure of the
body's defence resources.   It is argued, and this argument is
opposed by some, as will be shown later, that this stage may be
associated with the development of psychosomatic diseases, e.g.
gastric ulcer, cardiovascular diseases, colitis, etc.   It is
suggested that the tendency to develop a specific psychosomatic
disease is determined by pre-conditioning of some "target organ"
in the individual, by such factors as heredity, personal habits,
diet, previous exposure, or the specific actions of the causative
stress (e.g. a burn leading to a spreading skin ulcer).

It would appear further (Selye, 1960) that certain diseases
occur not primarily because of any specific pathogen or trauma but
because of a faulty adaptive response to the stressor effect of
some relatively harmless pathogen.   For example, various
emotional disturbances, headaches, insomnia, abdominal disorders,
etc., as well as recognised entities such as rheumatoid arthritis,
or certain allergic diseases, and sundry cardiovascular and renal
diseases, are alleged to be initiated not directly by some external
agency but as a result of faulty adaptive reactions (Selye, 1974).

In summary, then, it will be observed that human stress exists
when an event or state occurs which disturbs homeostasis.   The
extent of the resulting response, or strain, is determined by the

severity of the stress.   The response is non-specific and it
occurs regardless of the nature of the stress.   It is mediated via
the neuro-endocrine system and can be categorised in three stages of
adaptation: the stage of alarm, the stage of resistance and the
stage of exhaustion.   Faulty adaptation to the stress or failure
of the resistive mechanism is alleged to lead to disease.   A given
form of stress may in addition generate a specific response
superimposed upon the non-specific.   In some situations, e.g. the
acute stress of exposure to extreme environments, the specific
reactions, which are compensatory in nature, may overshadow the non-
specific.   Psychosocial stress, however, induces a non-specific
response.

THE NEEDS AND SATISFACTIONS OF WORK

4

Nature and history of work

The concept of work as an entity, independent of the needs of
day-to-day living, is one that is perhaps unique to post-industrial
societies. Primitive man was concerned with survival - hunting,
fishing, fundamental agriculture and the social and religious
rituals that accompanied these aspects of his life. Even in the
pre-industrial age, except for the few who could afford leisure,
work on the land or among the crafts and trades was still for most
a dawn-to-dusk way of life.

With the advent of industrialisation and specifically with the
Industrial Revolution came the realisation that work could in fact
be distinguished from other aspects of living, although the distinction is not always clear-cut. One man's work can be another man's
play. The athlete on the football field or the advertising agent
entertaining stars of the stage and screen may get very well paid
for work which is the envy of others engaged in more mundane activities. In fact, the situation in which the distinction between work
and leisure is the least clear-cut is commonly that in which the
greatest enjoyment is found by the worker. There are of course
exceptions and one can soon get tired of entertaining celebrities.
Most of what is regarded as work, in fact, tends to have connotations
of compulsion, either self-induced or applied from the exterior, and
involves the expenditure of time and effort on activities other than
those of one's personal desire. In its simplest form, work is what
one gets paid for, in currency or other consideration.

In his Report to the International Labour Conference in 1975,
Francis Blanchard, the Director-General of the ILO, pointed out that

the traditional views about work are being subjected more and more
to question:

> The most widespread view in the industrialised societies
> is that remunerated work - normally performed within an employ-
> ment relationship - is still the main means of personal fulfil-
> ment.   According to this view, questions relating to the
> organisation, content and hours of work are fundamental, just
> as is the extent to which the persons mainly involved partici-
> pate or not in decisions concerning an activity which is so
> essential to them.

> An entirely different attitude leads to such questions as:
> Is not work merely a constraint or even a necessary evil?   Is
> it not merely a means, from the personal point of view, of
> enabling us to earn a living and to do more interesting things
> in our free time?

> According to this view work should be merely an
> interruption in one's free time.   It should be reduced to a
> minimum (from the point of view of the individual) and made as
> efficient as possible (from the point of view of society),
> while the question of job satisfaction should be considered not
> in relation to work itself but in relation to the other objec-
> tives in life.

These two viewpoints of course represent the extremes, and like
any extremes they serve to define the boundaries.   Neither viewpoint
is completely tenable in our industrialised society, but while in the
past our efforts have been oriented towards the former, it must be
recognised that there is an increasing trend developing towards the
latter.

Development of industrialisation

The conflicting viewpoints derive from the very nature of the
process of industrialisation and the ultimate nature of industrialism.
Slotkin (1960), quoted by Carlestam and Levi (1971), points out that
industrialism is a set of interdependent customs, or phenomena, comprising the use of technological equipment which can neither be owned
nor operated by a single worker, as well as extensive division of
labour, formal industrial organisation, and interdependence between
the industrial organisation and the wider society.   He notes that
one or more of these characteristics may be found in other productive
systems, and particularly in the process of manufacturing, but in
none are the characteristics developed to such a high degree.

Historically, the process of industrialisation was closely
linked to organisational changes in agriculture, notably the development of larger agricultural units which in turn facilitated new
methods of cultivation, increased food production and more rapid

population growth.   The combination of these effects formed a base
for the subsequent process of industrialisation.

Concomitant with the development of industrialisation came the
development of transportation and communication, opening new markets
and stimulating the need for mass manufacture.   With the need for
mass manufacture came the beginnings of technology and ultimately
the far-reaching changes in the economic, social and physical
environment which are now taxing the adaptive capacities of man to
their limit.

Delamotte and Walker (1973), in a paper devoted to the humanisation of work, noted that among the significant changes wrought by
the Industrial Revolution, not only was there a mechanisation of
tasks which had previously been manual but also, and perhaps more
significantly from a social viewpoint, there was a change in thinking from the human-oriented to the machine-oriented.   Man, who had
previously been the focus of activity, was relegated to being a
tender of machines, except for the fortunate few who retained executive authority.

This viewpoint was crystallised by the work of F.W. Taylor
(1856-1917) in the United States, who developed concepts of scientific management in which human function and performance were regarded
as quantifiable and controllable variables.   Carpentier (1974) has
recently presented, inter alia, an analysis of the principles
involved.

It is argued that for every task there is an ideal method which
can be predetermined.   Every function can be analysed into its component tasks, each of which can be so designed as to be capable of
performance by relatively unskilled labour.   Several principles can
thus be defined: firstly, the independence of conception, planning
and execution; secondly, the division and standardisation of tasks,
equipment and products; and thirdly, the interchangeability of
operators.

The division of job requirements and the standardisation of
low-level skills are designed to facilitate recruitment, while
minimising the personal role of the worker and limiting the risk of
error and, for that matter, of initiative.   The interchangeability
of operators is, of course, intended to ensure that the resulting
product is independent of the individuals involved in its production.
These requirements in turn lead to a need for supervisors, both of

quality and quantity, planning and co-ordination services and a
hierarchical structure.

Carpentier goes on to state: "Scientific concepts ... (of the
period) ... postulated a mechanistic determinism based on the
assumption that it was possible to analyse every detail of a system
and specify the precise requirements for its perfect theoretical
operation, independently of human intervention; moreover, these
concepts were applied to man himself, stressing the rational and
mechanical aspects of life."

From the point of view of productivity there is no doubt that
the approach and its implementation were effective, particularly at
a time when the workforce in the countries concerned was relatively
unsophisticated and still primarily concerned with seeking the
wherewithal for simple survival. This approach, however, success-
ful though it has been in material terms, has carried with it the
elements of its own destruction, in that the very productivity it
has engendered has permitted development of sophistication and knowledge amongst the workers, such that they are no longer prepared to
be mere mechanistic components of a manufacturing system but seek
instead recognition of their qualities and services as human beings.

Humanisation of work

This requirement for humanisation of work has, of course, been
recognised by the International Labour Office, as well as by other
international and national agencies and individuals (see Reports of
the ILO Director-General to the International Labour Conference, 1974,
1975). As far back as 1954, Dr. Lloyd-Davies argued eloquently that
while men can be conditioned, at least for a time, to meaningless
work, work that has no creative element is soul-destroying and
unworthy. He states (Lloyd-Davies, 1954) " ... Work, which should
not be confused with gainful employment, is the best, if not the sole,
means of bringing the individual into relation with events going on
around him ... The prime requirement of an industrial democracy is
that the work itself should be worthy of the dignity of a human
being." And while one might take issue with the first part of his
statement, it is difficult to argue with the latter.

Regardless of whether the criterion for humanusation is increase
in productivity or improvement in human well-being, the concept has
become established. At the 59th Session of the International Labour
Conference, 1974, a resolution was adopted calling for a global

approach to the working environment, and covering such matters as:
"protection against physical conditions and dangers at the workplace
and its immediate environment; adaptation of installations and work
processes to the physical and mental aptitudes of the worker through
the application of ergonomic principles; prevention of mental
stress due to the pace and monotony of work, and promotion of the
quality of working life through the amelioration of the conditions
of work, including job design and job content and related questions
of work organisation; the full participation of employers and
workers and their organisations in the elaboration, planning and
implementation of policies for the improvement of the working
environment".

One must not, of course, fall into the trap of confusing
humanisation of work with job satisfaction. Humanisation of work
is a concept which is applied to the physical, procedural and social
requirements of the working (operational) environment. Humanisation
seeks achievement of an ideal goal, and much has been written about
it. Not only is it concerned with improving the physical conditions
of the working environment and supervisory relationships; it is also
concerned with changing the nature of work itself, using techniques
such as job enlargement, work enrichment, job rotation (ILO, 1974 a)
or the sophisticated approaches to the reorganisation of work
attempted by such industries as Olivetti in Italy, Ferrodo in
Britain, BSN in France, Atlas Copco, Saab-Scania and Volvo in Sweden,
Fiat in the USSR, Rade Koncar in Yugoslavia, and Shell Canada in
Sarnia, etc.

Job satisfaction, on the other hand, is a subjective, personal
state perceived by the individual as being in his favour; and while
there is no doubt that humanisation of work may contribute to job
satisfaction, it should not be assumed that humanisation of work will
ensure the generation or the maintenance of job satisfaction. The
noted Hawthorne experiments of the 1920s and 1930s (Roethlisberger
and Dickson, 1939) showed that workers react to managerial interest,
but they also showed that once a desirable innovation in working conditions had been made and accepted there is a tendency to adopt the
new level as normal without any positive reaction of job satisfaction.
In fact, there are elements in programmes aiming at humanisation of
work that can have negative effects on individuals. The worker who
is contented with his working situation may not wish to accept responsibility, make decisions or influence supervisory practices.

Indeed, as is noted by Mansell (1980) of the Ontario Quality of Working Life Group, despite 20 years of effort to convince managers, unionists and workers of the advantages of new work forms, innovation within the workplace is still relatively rare. Some trade unionists would argue that new work forms based on greater employee participation for the purposes of improving job satisfaction could be used as a means of reducing union influence or increasing productivity within increasing pay (Barbash, 1977).

Philosophy and theories of
work satisfaction

Job satisfaction or, in its broader form, work satisfaction, is a difficult entity to define even in simplistic terms. For the individual worker, it exists when the perceived benefits of the work exceed the perceived costs by a margin deemed by the worker to be adequate under the circumstances. It is not, however, a static state and is subject to influence and modification from forces within and outside of the immediate work environment. One school of thought, in fact (Goldthorpe et al., 1968), examines the problem in terms of its extrinsic or intrinsic orientation, that is whether the worker is primarily concerned with work as a means to provide fulfilment outside of the job, or finds fulfilment in the work itself, the former perhaps tending to be more of a working-class value and the latter more of a middle-class one. Furthermore, job satisfaction is not the unitary or integrated state that the name would imply. There are multiple facets to the working state, some of which are more satisfying, or perhaps more acceptable, and others less. Job satisfaction at best describes in comparative terms some integrated mean of that state at some point in time. There is no absolute on some infinite scale. At best we can state that at this particular time one is more satisfied with some aspect of one's job than at some other time.

Regardless of the semantics, various approaches have been made towards defining basic work satisfaction.

Numerous authors have generated lists of characteristics considered to be desirable in the attainment of satisfaction at work (e.g. Margolis, Kroes and Quinn, 1974; Slawina and Moykin, 1975; Taylor, 1974; Vamplew, 1973; Johnston, 1973, 1975; Hill, 1973; Johnston and Gherardi, 1970), but the original organisation from

which many contemporary views has evolved owes much to the work of
Maslow and of Herzberg, despite the fact that their theories were
largely developed from study of limited levels of society.
Maslow's theoretical model postulates the existence in man of
primary and secondary drives which serve to motivate him (Maslow,
1954). He argues that the primary drives are inherited, although
the means for satisfying them can be learned. The primary drives
stem from physiological needs and are oriented towards survival.
They include basic appetites such as hunger, thirst and sex. The
secondary drives are not inherited but are learned and, to some
extent at least, they may be culturally determined. They include
such requirements as security, manifested in a need for protection
and freedom from fear, as well as a requirement for organised
structure, law and order. A need for love, affection and a sense
of group identity, or belonging, is also defined. A third group
comprises the need for self-esteem, represented by a desire for
self-assurance, confidence and mastery along with feelings of
achievement and the need for establishment of reputation and prestige. Maslow also defines a concept of self-actualisation or the
need to become more fully developed and to reify one's ideals.

The lower order needs, particularly the primary drives and
the need for security and structure, are very largely met in
today's industrial society. It is argued that what is needed now
is satisfaction of the higher order needs, notably those pertaining to self-esteem and self-actualisation, to use Maslow's terms.
And, in fact, it is only in a society where the lower order needs
have been largely met that people can afford to seek satisfaction
of the higher order.

Herzberg (1966), from his work, has in fact stated that the
main factors involved in job satisfaction are advancement, recognition, responsibility, growth and the job itself. These factors,
termed "satisfiers", will correlate, if optimised, with improved
performance, reduced labour turnover, more tolerant attitudes to
management, and general "mental health". Herzberg also recognises "dissatisfiers", which act in a negative direction. These
include such things as working conditions and amenities, administrative policies, relationship with supervisors, technical compe-
tence of supervisors, pay, job security and relationship with
peers. Herzberg argues that if the quality of the "dissatisfiers"
is less than adequate, dissatisfaction will occur. Improvement

in the degraded condition or conditions will remove the dissatisfaction with beneficial effects on morale and perhaps on productivity. Raising the level above the adequate, however, will
not of itself increase job satisfaction and performance, but it
will provide a basis for the potential fulfilment of the "higher
needs" defined by Maslow (1954). In this regard it should be
noted that much of Herzberg's work was conducted among supervisors
and middle-management employees, as so much motivational research
has indeed been done. How much it is applicable to the worker on
the shop floor is open to question.

Vroom, cited by Hunt (1971), adds another dimension to job
satisfaction theory. He argues that the choice of a job initially
depends upon what he refers to as "first-level outcome", namely
money or direct reward. Behind the first-level outcome, and perceived by the worker with greater or less clarity, are second-level
outcomes which may be inherent in the job, such as prestige and
power, or may be attainable by way of the money provided as a first-
level outcome. The effort that the worker is willing to expend,
and the satisfaction that he derives in doing so, are directly
related to the strength of the second-level goals and the clarity
of the perceived relationship between the primary and the secondary
goals. Expectancy is a third factor. The higher the expectancy
of the secondary goal, as perceived by the worker, the greater is the
perceived worth of the primary, and hence the satisfaction derived in
attaining it.

Expounding on an analysis earlier presented by Gilmer (1961),
the approach of Fox (1971) is representative of another, more operationally oriented viewpoint on job satisfaction. He defines three
fields of concern in job satisfaction, namely content of the job
(i.e. skills), context of the job (i.e. the network of structure and
reward within which the worker functions), and the needs of the
incumbent. In terms of desirable job content he refers to skills
that require qualities ofperception, motor co-ordination, intellect
and education, and provide opportunity for creative expression and
flexibility of response. The structural context of the job includes
the financial rewards, the location of the work, the nature of the
workloads and the adequacy of the equipment. More intangible
factors are security of tenure, prospects for promotion, justice in
promotion, and company attitudes, while the company structure
itself, its planning policy and reputation are also significant.

In the area of supervisory and peer relationships competent supervision, co-operation and communication through the hierarchy is
important, while outside the actual task environment the provision
of recreational resources is significant.   He defines the needs of
the incumbent in personal and social terms akin to the higher order
drives of Maslow or the "satisfiers" of Herzberg, namely the
requirement for recognition of one's own value and the need for
creative drive and fulfilment.   He recognises that there must be
orientation towards a personal goal with, however, an awareness of
the system of priorities within which one may be permitted to achieve
it.   The individual must at the same time possess an appropriate
level of physical and mental energy to achieve his ends, along
with the capacity to conform, where required, and to tolerate
stress.   For many, there is also a need for social involvement.

Barbash (1974) has argued, with some justification, that job
satisfaction is seen to be different things by different people,
and that specifically the search for job satisfaction is not
primarily a "grass-roots" movement demanded by the worker but a
practice imposed from the top by intellectuals and liberalised
management.   "There is a strong likelihood ... ", he states,
" ... that full employment and its attendant conditions have more
to do with workers' free choice than either management policy or
the internal environment of the undertaking."   To put it another
way, where there is an expectancy of full employment then the
primary drives defined by Maslow are likely to be satisfied and
the worker can afford to allow himself to be concerned with Maslow's
higher order drives or Herzberg's "satisfiers".   When there is no
expectancy of full employment the needs of survival become paramount - a phenomenon which has been exploited since man first went
to work for his fellow man.

Singleton (1979), in an essay dealing with conceptual and
operational doubts about job satisfaction, issues a word of warning
when he describes the concern with job satisfaction as an
"ideological/political movement", and points out that such move-
ments should be treated cautiously.   He goes on to state: "They
are sometimes no more than fashionable crusades and there is a
perpetual danger that such crusades will result in overemphasis on
a particular facet of the complex multidimensional problems of work
design which is encompassed by ergonomics."   He goes on to add
that nevertheless politicians and ideologists do sometimes
crystallise a fundamental trend in thinking.

Job dissatisfaction - extent of the problem

Before examining specific factors associated with satisfaction
and dissatisfaction, it is pertinent to consider whether in fact
there is a problem which can be attributed to lack of job satisfaction.   There is a tendency to assume that if working, social
and other conditions are unsuitable, then dissatisfaction must
exist and that this in turn is an undesirable state, both for the
worker and for the employer.   But is it in fact a problem?   Very
few researchers have addressed themselves to this question.   Kahn
(1972) cited by Barbash (1974) has noted that few people call themselves extremely satisfied with their jobs, but still fewer report
extreme dissatisfaction.   The majority claim to be reasonably
satisfied.   In an analysis of the meagre literature on the subject,
Barbash (1974) observes from a US Senate Survey that 20 per cent of
people will always dislike work regardless of how it is organised.
A United Kingdom report places dissatisfaction in the area of
5 per cent, while two Japanese surveys show 23 per cent and 15 per
cent respectively.   Gilmer (1961) suggests the average is about
13 per cent.   But, even taking the highest of these figures to
represent the dissatisfied body, it would appear that the great
majority of workers are indeed reasonably satisfied.   But do the
figures represent reality?   This is where the question still
remains unanswered.   The data are very inadequate and insufficient
for use as a base for drawing definitive conclusions.   The
observers, the experts and the commentators on the working scene
consider that there is a problem.   And there probably is.   A
fairly large majority, though inarticulate in their expression,
are probably to a greater or lesser extent dissatisfied, although
only a minority are prepared to voice their dissatisfaction and
attempt to do something about it.

Whatever the extent of the dissatisfaction, and whatever its
significance, there is no doubt that it exists in some form, and
that its cause can, to some extent at least, be defined.   A paper
presented to the High Authority of the European Coal and Steel
Community in Luxembourg (1967) stated: "A worker starts making
comparisons between his training, his position in the undertaking,
the more or less demanding nature of his work, his earnings, and so
on, and becomes convinced that he is badly off in his particular
job."

The broad causes of dissatisfaction, of course, are not hard to find. They lie in failure to meet the requirements for satisfaction that were examined above. In 1974 the Director-General of the International Labour Office, in summarising these with a broad sweep, has stated:

> Far too many workers are in dead-end jobs, requiring the exercise of little or no initiative or responsibility, with few prospects of advancement or mobility to other types of work. Far too many workers perform tasks which are far below their intellectual capacity, and which they consider to be degrading in relation to the education which they have received. In many industries and occupations, work has been "rationalised" to an extreme, broken down into simple, negative and monotonous jobs which are fit for an unthinking robot, but which are an insult to the dignity, the aspirations and the cultural level of twentieth century man.

There can be little doubt that such a working environment constitutes stress, but how in fact is it perceived by the worker?

Specific factors involved in job satisfaction

It is frequently difficult to obtain a clear view of the personal priorities and evaluations of workers from the established literature. Most, if not all, attitude surveys rely on some form of questionnaire, in which the designer has pre-empted the questions and the areas of interest, normally of course with sound justification, but often oriented more to the negative than to the positive. The responder, however, then addresses himself to the questions that are asked and not necessarily to the points that are specifically contentious to him, nor to what he finds good about this work.

Thus in interpreting surveys one must recognise that to some extent at least the survey may incorporate some of the originator's prejudices. Sometimes, of course, viewpoints on attitudes are expressed, ex cathedra as it were, on the basis of experience and knowledge. Thus Ling (1954), for example, from the empirical standpoint of the industrial physician, claimed, on the basis of his observation and experience, that there are six types of goal that must be achieved before satisfaction can be attained. These, he claimed, are money, prestige and status, security, approval, a sense of belonging, and creativeness. He preceded Vroom when he pointed out that the effectiveness of money as a source of satisfaction depends on the extent to which it can be used to satisfy real needs. He distinguished between prestige and status, pointing out that the

former is earned in proportion to the contribution made while the
latter may be a function of the job.   Security and approval are
closely related and imply an opportunity for advancement, while for
proper work satisfaction the worker also requires a feeling of group
identity.   The term "creativity" in the sense that Ling used it
referred not so much to the art of creating as to the feeling that
what one is doing is significant in itself.

Herzberg (cited by Gilmer, 1961) conducted some 150 or more
studies to come to somewhat similar conclusions, although the order
of priority is somewhat different. He lists, in order of importance,
security or steadiness of employment, opportunity for advancement,
the worker's perception of the company and its management, salary,
the intrinsic aspects of the job itself, the quality of the supervision, the social aspects of the job, the quality of communication, i.e. the extent to which workers are involved in communication, physical working conditions and hours of work, and the extent
of benefits.

Now it should be recognised that these requirements are being
reported by employees who are already for the most part, if not
entirely, working under conditions which are reasonably tolerable,
where wages are higher than starvation level, and supervisory
relations, while not perhaps of the best, are certainly not on a
master-slave basis.   This viewpoint is confirmed by other more
recent studies.

Ruth Johnston (1975), for example, in addition to reporting
her own work, reviewed a number of studies of worker attitudes
which serve to emphasise the relative unimportance of money and
physical conditions when these have, at least to some extent, been
dealt with.   In some of her initial work among workers in a soap
factory where 80 per cent of the workforce claimed to be satisfied
(Johnston and Gherardi, 1970), she demonstrated a rank order
preference among males for an interesting job, friendly co-workers,
an efficient and interested management, good pay and kind supervision.   In females, in the same study, the rank preference was
for friendly co-workers, an interesting job with kind supervision,
an efficient and interested management and good pay.

In a subsequent study among union members in the construction
industry (Johnston, 1973), in which 62 per cent claimed satisfaction, workers again rated friendliness and job interest as
preferential characteristics.   Similar findings have been observed

elsewhere, even amongst the unemployed. Hill and associates (1973) showed in a study of unemployment in three English towns that unemployed men in urban areas listed the qualities of desirable jobs as the need for interesting and satisfying work, good pay, a good supervisor, good working conditions and satisfactory co-workers, while Lloyd-Davies (1954) demonstrated that 55 per cent of young males and 15 per cent of young females beginning work in an industrial and commercial organisation gave as their major reasons for selecting that organisation the presence of friends and relations (32 per cent), good company reputation (19 per cent) and the known work conditions (4 per cent).

Even the stress of unemployment, however, can elicit a positive response. Little (1973) conducted a study on unemployment as a psychosocial stress. He compared the responses of 100 unemployed technical professionals with a group of technical professionals. The strain measures included internally oriented manifestations of self-blame, psychosomatic disorder, depression and irritability, along with externally oriented responses directed to the economic conditions, management, and the administration. In this study the unemployed subjects showed a greater response to stress than did the employed subjects. In a later study, however (Little, 1978), among engineers in the aerospace industry, he reported that many of the unemployed viewed their position as an opportunity rather than a catastrophe, particularly among those at the beginning of their careers in situations where job satisfaction was low. In this connection, however, it must be realised that fluidity of jobs is commonplace in the US aerospace industry.

The significance of money and payment as a motivating force is difficult to assess, in that the stated views of the workers on money and financial reward seem to be somewhat inconsistent, and may even be industry-specific. According to Walker and Guest (1952), workers in the automobile industry are almost exclusively concerned with money, whereas most other surveys, with a few exceptions, consider money as a significant but not necessarily primary factor in job choice and job satisfaction. The automobile industry, of course, is in general one in which there are certainly many problems related to the working conditions and environment. Argyle (1972), cited by Johnston (1975), quotes studies suggesting that when other variables such as the physical conditions of work, job content, quality of supervision, and social relations are held

constant, then financial reward correlates with over-all job satisfaction at the relatively low level of 0.25.   However,
in assessing the relative value of money as a motivating factor in
job satisfaction, even along the previously described lines suggested by Vroom, it must be recognised that the reported data on
attitudes to money are open to interpretation.   Money, as part of
a reward system, has emotional connotations.   To some, regardless
of the job, money is a goal; to others money may be secondary,
while to all their attitude may be coloured by the views of the
culture in which they have developed.   Vamplew (1973) reports on
the attitude of workers in the automated chemical industry, who
showed a high degree of job satisfaction, related to interest in
their work, a feeling of achievement and recognition of their
qualities.   Any dissatisfaction that occurred was occasioned by
technical failures and, paradoxically, an element of boredom when
everything went well.   Nevertheless, in assessing the qualities of
their job 92 per cent rated the pay as the most important consideration followed by security, interest and responsibility, and all gave
strong support to the posture of their union.   Vamplew attributes
this somewhat unexpected stance to the fact that while the occupations surveyed were of a responsible nature, the background and
culture of the workers led them to pursue the traditional worker's
values.

The system of payment itself may also be a source of satisfaction or dissatisfaction, and various approaches, outside of the
scope of this study, are being taken towards its solution (ILO,
1974 c).   The requirements of duration of work, shift work and
night work are also commonly cited as a source of dissatisfaction
(ILO, 1974 a; WHO, 1972; ILO, 1974 c).   While these are of psychosocial interest, their effects of course are also of physiological
interest because of the resultant disturbance of circadian cycles
and subsequent direct contribution to clinical disturbance.   These
effects will be examined in a later chapter.

Special consideration needs to be given also to the **unique**
relationships of job satisfaction in migrant workers, but again that
would appear to be outside the scope of this particular study.   For
a review in this area one is referred to Levi and Anderson (1974,
pp. 66-70).

Job satisfaction and safety

A discussion of job satisfaction cannot be left, however, without at least some reference to the relationship between job satisfaction and safety. Very little in fact has been recorded demonstrating such a relationship, although the safety literature is replete with examinations of the motivations that may underlie safe or unsafe behaviour; many of these motivations indeed are identical with those which give rise to the subjective reaction of job dissatisfaction. In a paper delivered to the European Community on Coal and Steel (CECA, 1967) already noted, the author of the paper observes that the dissatisfied worker acquired a conviction that he is at a disadvantage in comparison with others. He goes on to note that if this conviction is established it becomes a latent dissatisfaction which is externalised in a lack of care and attention.

This lack of care and attention can of course result in accidents. Neuloh et al. (1957) found firstly a higher incidence of accidents among workers who had been moved from a job which they perceived to be good to a job which they considered to be poorer or less prestigious. Secondly, among skilled workers where the worker was exercising his trade, one worker in 20 became an accident victim, while if a skilled worker were not exercising his trade, one worker in six or seven was a victim.

With respect to relations with co-workers, where good relations existed one worker in 20 had an accident, but where relations were bad one worker in ten had an accident.

Other confirmatory evidence showing the relationship between job satisfaction and accidents was provided by Kerr (1950) who showed that under the circumstances examined, the majority of accidents tended to occur where there was the least possibility of advancement.

Thus, while there is little in the way of direct evidence to show a cause and effect relationship between job dissatisfaction and accidents, the evidence is suggestive. It would appear that where conditions exist such as to reduce job satisfaction there is a greater tendency towards accidents.

THE PSYCHOPHYSIOLOGY OF WORK AND FATIGUE

5

In the previous chapter, consideration has been given to the nature of job satisfaction, and the requirements of work. It has been shown that man has various drives and satisfaction needs, some of which can be satisfied by work, and its rewards. The material has been examined largely from a psychosocial point of view. To understand more fully, however, the relationships that exist among work, job satisfaction and human stress, it is desirable to examine the psychophysiology of work and fatigue.

From the point of view of physiology, two different forms of work can be distinguished, namely work that primarily requires muscular strength (physical work), and work that primarily requires skill or intellect (skilled work). The physiological mechanisms in each case are different. Virtually all activities, of course, involve some mix of physical and skilled attributes. Singling them out for examination has to be done with this realisation.

Physical work

Physical work involves muscle contraction against a load. The energy required for the contraction is derived from the progressive chemical breakdown or oxidation of sugars and starches ingested in the diet or stored in the body, with the eventual production of water, carbon dioxide and sundry end products or metabolites. The blood circulation brings oxygen and materials to the site of the action and removes carbon dioxide and waste products for eventual elimination.

Energy is required, of course, to a greater or less extent, for the function of all other body processes. From the physical viewpoint the body is a moderately efficient heat engine which does

work and produces heat.   The heat produced is measurable in kilo-
calories (kcal) and is representative of the energy expenditure.
For the basic energy expenditure of living, i.e. at total rest,
fasting, in a thermoneutral environment, the basal metabolic rate
of the average man is considered to be about 1,750 kcal per day,
while the average energy expenditure over an extended period of
light industrial work, including basal expenditure, is considered
to be about 3,200 kcal per day.   It is also generally accepted
that the maximum output for extended periods should not exceed
4,800 kcal per day (Lehmann, 1958).   This figure, also presented
as approximately 5 kcal per minute, is echoed by Murrell (1965) in
a review of other studies.   Should work continue at or beyond
these levels for more than a few weeks or months there will be progressive reduction in performance, absenteeism and sickness, as was
shown for example by studies in Britain during the First and Second
World Wars.   (Note reports of the Industrial Fatigue Research
Board, Great Britain.)   It is uncommon today, however, to find
organised industry where workers even approach these levels of
energy expenditure, with the possible exception of coalminers
(3,500-4,000 kcal per working day for a working life) and Canadian
lumberjacks (5,000-5,500 kcal per day for two to three months per
year).   The process of fatigue, however, even in muscular work,
is relatively little understood and even less well defined.   The
acute fatigue of heavy muscular work, associated with pain and
stiffness of limbs, generalised weariness and desire for sleep, is
no doubt associated with accumulation of acid metabolites in the
muscles, local disturbance of electrolyte balance, inflammatory
swelling of muscle fibres within their sheaths and depletion of
immediate energy reserves.   In addition, it is suggested that
metabolites trigger impulses to subcortical and cortical centres in
the brain, with resulting inhibition of motor areas and decrease in
the frequency of activity of motor neurons (Edholm, 1967).   The
total fatigue mechanism of muscular exercise, however, is probably
much more complex, involving changes in information processing
capacity and output from the brain, perhaps changes in neural transmission, reduction in energy transforming capacity, changes in the
capacity to acquire, transport and utilise oxygen, etc.

Even when not working at his limit, however, a worker will
seek and use rest pauses, whether those pauses comprise actual
stoppage of work, as for a coffee or lunch break, or a change in
the workload or quality of work, such as cleaning the surrounds of

a bench between work cycles.   In an extensive review of the subject, Murrell (1965) discusses the relative significance of actual
work stoppage in comparison with introduction of variety in the type
of work during a given period, or the reorganisation of workload
during a given period, observing that if appropriate breaks are not
officially prescribed by management, efficiency will decrease and
dissatisfaction increase; or that workers will effect disguised
breaks, or utilise work-conditioned breaks by taking advantage of
the external pacing of the work.   With an appropriate schedule of
breaks, the frequency and duration of which are determined by the
job, output and attitude will both improve.

It will be clear, then, that physical work, if sufficiently
severe to encroach on human limits, can indeed constitute a severe
stress.   It is also apparent, however, that physical work of much
lesser severity, if pursued during the working day without a break,
can also constitute a stress.   In each case the stress is minimised
by appropriate rest pauses or work change.

Skilled work

The question of skilled work, and the fatigue that is associated
with it, is still more complex, and in fact that concepts of skill,
arousal, boredom, fatigue and stress seem to be inextricably inter-
linked.   In a comprehensive review, Cameron (1973) has stated:
"Fatigue has generally been considered in simple mechanistic terms,
in some way similar to the depletion of a fixed amount of energy,
as in the running down of a fly-wheel or the discharge of an elec-
trical storage battery.   The published reports on the topic indicate
that this naive conceptualisation is present implicitly in much of the
previous work, although the results of experimental studies are not
consistent with it.   There seems to have been a failure to realise
that fatigue is a complex biological phenomenon.   The human is both
adaptive and purposive in his behaviour; if the demands of his task
are high, he can respond with great effort; if the incentives to
continue working are high, he can maintain this effort over a very
long period.   He also responds to the stimulation provided by an
interesting or challenging task."

Skill itself is difficult to define.   Murrell (1965) has
recognised five categories of skilled industrial task which may or
may not be combined in one job.   These involve, firstly, repetitive
work, where the same sequence of operations is expected to be

repeated; secondly, monitoring, which is the circumstance under
which an inactive individual is expected to watch for longer or
shorter periods of time for signals which may occur at infrequent
intervals; thirdly, driving, which applies not only to vehicles
but to other types of control systems such as cranes or rolling
mills; fourthly, machine minding, where the worker tends semi-
automatic or automatic machines; and finally, inspection, which is
concerned with examination, gauging and perhaps measuring a product.

To look at the nature of skill itself, however, one has to
turn to more experimental evidence, and particularly the theories
developed by Bartlett and others on the work of the Cambridge
Cockpit Studies (Davis, 1946; Drew, 1940; Bartlett, 1943), still
cited as classical. These studies involved observations and performance measurements on pilots operating for several hours at a
stretch in a simulated aircraft flying in rough air. Several
findings emerged: with the passage of time during a flight, the
pilots showed a diminution in their range of attention, along with
an acceptance of lowered personal standards of accuracy and performance; in addition the pilots demonstrated progressive failure to
integrate flight instruments as a unit, or in other words failed to
cross-correlate information with the object of deriving new information; there was also a failure to maintain the hierarchy of previously established priorities of information management and action,
i.e. there was a tendency for activity to be directed towards
"putting out fires"; and there was loss of immediate memory for
information from peripheral instruments.

To generalise these findings into a theory of skill and skill
fatigue, it is argued that the worker performing a skilled task,
be it flying, monitoring a console, or tending a milling machine,
perceives his task as a whole, in relation to the environment in
which he is operating. The individual components and subcomponents
of that task and that environment are constantly changing, but the
stimuli are perceived as a total pattern. Thus the arrangement and
value of individual stimuli may change without degrading the total
pattern, in the same manner that a waterfall is constantly changing
yet retains its total pattern.

The skilled operator sees his task in terms of the total
integrated pattern of stimuli. Consciously or unconsciously he
sets up subjective standards or limits, based on learned behaviour,

for permissible variation in individual stimuli, and in the pattern
as a whole, and performs his task within these terms of reference.
With prolonged attention to the task, and depending on other
intrinsic and extrinsic factors, a state of acute fatigue will
develop. The standards subjectively established by the operator
will be allowed to deteriorate, the timing of actions will become
disorganised, i.e. the operator may do the right action out of phase
with the need; the stimulus field subjectively organised by the
operator splits and disintegrates and the previously determined
pattern becomes a collection of disconnected signals each requiring
action, some more immediately than others. In addition the peripheral demands of the task, those that are not closely organised,
tend to become overlooked. Initially the phenomenon is momentary,
but with time the lapses increase in duration. Initially also
they can be relieved by extra effort but eventually even the extra
effort is no longer adequate and performance fails. At first the
phenomenon tends to be specific to the task at hand and can be
relieved by changing the activity or the demands, but with change
it begins to build anew and become progressive to other skills until
it can only be relieved by rest. Subjectively the condition is
associated with lassitude, weariness and an unwillingness to continue with the task.

The foregoing is descriptive of the subjective reaction, and
at least some of the mechanisms involved, but by no means comprises
a definition. Some people claim in fact that fatigue defies precise definition. Bartlett (1953) gives the operational definition
that fatigue refers to " ... those determinable changes in the
expression of the activity which can be traced to the continued
exercise of that activity under its normal operational conditions,
and which can be shown to lead ... to results within the activity
which are not wanted ... ". As a definition, however, this is
probably so broad as to be of limited practical value. Cameron
(1973) considers, in fact, that fatigue is a useful label for a
generalised response to stress over a period of time, which has
identifiable and measurable characteristics, but no explanatory
value. In other words, Cameron, with considerable justification,
equates fatigue with stress (or, by the definition used here, with
strain), a fact of some significance in considering stress and job
satisfaction.

The relationship becomes more obvious when one examines chronic
fatigue which is the condition that arises by the relatively slow
process of accumulation of fatigue.   Bartley and Chute (cited by
Cameron, 1973) who originated the concept of chronic fatigue,
observed that in contrast to acute fatigue chronic fatigue is progressive and is not relieved by the normal processes of rest.
Ross McFarland (1971), who has done extensive work with fatigue in
air crew, observes that in fact chronic fatigue is a psychological
or psychiatric problem characterised by boredom, loss of initiative
and progressive anxiety, which may be either a cause or an effect
of stress, and that the boredom which may be a feature may also be
a cause.

The question of boredom leads to consideration of the concept
of arousal and its relationship to boredom, fatigue and stress.
Since the original work of Moruzzi and Magoun (1949), the concept
of arousal and its mechanisms has become fairly well established.
Arousal refers to a state of alertness maintained by centres deep
in the brain.   Arousal may be evoked by some stimulus which origi-
nates in the environment, is transmitted by the sensory nervous
system to higher centres in the brain where it is perceived as a
change or even a threat and causes subsequent transmission of
alerting signals to the arousal centres.   These in turn transmit
further nerve signals which, as it were, increase the sensitivity
of the nervous system and maintain the state of alertness.   Arousal
can also be maintained by signals arising directly from the cortex
of the brain without environmental origin, for example from thought
or emotion.   Normally there is a certain basic level of activity
which may be increased or reduced.

Arousal tends to be maintained for some 10-20 minutes from the
time of the initial stimulus.   If it is not then reinforced by a
further or new stimulus, opening a new loop, the arousal will reduce
to the relaxed base-line state, perhaps from progressive failure of
transmission across the synapses, or nerve fibre junctions, from
exhaustion of transmitter substance.

In addition to the arousal system there is also an inhibitory
system first described by Hess (1927), who observed that stimulation
of what is now known to be a portion of the reticular formation
would cause an animal to fall asleep.   Grandjean (1968) has pointed
out that the two systems work in opposition, and that a person's

ability to perform a task is dependent on the relative degree of
activity of the two systems.   Where the inhibitory system
dominates, the organism is in a state subjectively experienced as
the lassitude of fatigue, although the subject may or may not show
other biochemical or physiological evidence of fatigue.   If the
activating system is dominant he is in a state of arousal.   Activation tends to be stimulated by external factors, e.g. sensation,
perception, conscious awareness, whereas inhibition occurs as a
post-stress phenomenon associated with depleted resources.   Inhibition also occurs, however, in the absence of external stimuli where
the environment itself lacks stimulation.

This concept goes far in explaining some of the apparent
paradoxes of fatigue: how it can disappear in excitement or
danger, how it can occur readily in conditions of boredom and monotony, how the very act of trying to measure it causes it to diminish,
and how stress itself can be both a cause and an effect of fatigue.

Stress, of course, is not confined to the situation in which
some undesirable element is added to the environment.   As Heron and
his colleagues have shown in their classic experiments in sensory
deprivation, extreme stress can arise when an environment is devoid
of stimulation (Heron, 1961; Doane et al., 1959).

In the industrial situation, of course, sensory deprivation
does not occur, but there are indeed conditions which tend to produce inhibition of the reticular activating system, and hence
reduced arousal, reduced alertness, and reduced vigilance, subjectively experienced as monotony, boredom and fatigue.   Basically
these conditions arise where the work is lacking in inherent
interest and motivating capacity, and where there is a minimal
demand on the operator within an inherently dull environment.   Conditions are aggravated further where the worker is engaged in
continuously repetitive work, or is exposed to long periods of
vigilance with little action.   Many of these undesirable features
are found in machine-paced assembly work, but some of the more
unusual situations have occurred among individuals working alone
in "clean rooms" and have resulted in dramatic emotional and psychosomatic disturbances.

The extent to which stress is implicated in the generation of
dissatisfaction, emotional disturbance and psychosomatic disorder
will be examined in the next chapter.

STRESS MECHANISMS AND MANIFESTATIONS IN WORK

6

Work as a stressor

It has already been noted that stress exists whenever there is a change in the equilibrium of a man-machine-environment complex. Since the complex is an interactive system, the stress so generated is distributed among the components of the system; since man, from the operational and anthropometric viewpoints, is the weakest component of the system, then commonly some or all of the resulting strain is manifested in some human response. Thus, to recapitulate, as stress occurs within the physical, occupational or social components of the operational environment which may commonly result in a manifestation of human strain. The stress may be generated by various stressors, simple or complex. The question that arises is to what extent that stress is implicated in the generation of dissatisfaction, emotional disturbance and psychosomatic disorder.

It is already well established, and supported by an enormous literature, that specific elements such as noise, heat, cold and numerous other potentially intolerable conditions constitute stressors within the working environment, and it can be accepted without any doubt that where such conditions exist there will be stress, greater or less dissatisfaction, and a greater or less effect on productivity and performance. It has also been shown that within a very high level of motivation in a selected population such as the military, astronauts or cosmonauts, a very high level of performance can be maintained despite conditions that would normally be considered intolerable, with less irreversible strain. In fact, one might speculate, although it has not been formally proved, that in conditions of stress there is a strong negative correlation between level of motivation and resulting pathology.

A civilian worker, however, is not an astronaut; his motivations
are less clearly oriented, particularly where his immediate survival
is not at stake.   Also, in most recent cases at least, his capacity
to adapt to or accept stress is less highly developed.

Theory of work stress

Some researchers (e.g., Lazarus, 1967) maintain that stress
refers only to those transactions with the environment that involve
harm or threat of harm, and that the main relevant emotions include
fear, anxiety, guilt, anger, grief, depression and disgust.   This
viewpoint of course is valid in so far as it goes, but it is
predicated on the subjective perception of something harmful, and
tends to be somewhat atomistic in its approach.   The holistic
view, which sees stress as something which tends to disturb homeostasis, was of course propounded by Selye, as already noted, and
goes far in explaining the relationship between stress and work.
Dr. Levi and his associates at the Laboratory for Clinical Stress
Research in Sweden have been among the foremost in investigating
this relationship, and have opened for consideration the whole field
of psychosocially induced disorder or disease, which in turn has its
counterpart in psychosomatic medicine.

Sweetland (1979), in a review of some 100 pieces of literature,
notes that theoretical models can provide a useful framework for
analysis of the relationship between stress and productivity.   By
inference, these models can also provide a useful framework for
analysis of the relationship between stress and work satisfaction.
Thus, according to Wilford (1973), stress arises when there is a
deviation from optimum conditions that cannot be easily corrected,
causing an imbalance between demand and capacity.   The most widely
accepted model to define this relationship is the "inverted-U"
hypothesis, which indicates that performance improves with increasing
stress to a certain level beyond which, as stress continues to
increase, the performance declines.

Anderson (1976) showed evidence of this relationship in the
behaviour of 102 owner-managers of small businesses damaged in a
hurricane.   He viewed the mechanism in terms of "signal detection"
theory, in which the brain is considered to act to discriminate meaningful signals from random ones.   The individual establishes some
threshold above which signals of importance will be received, the
remainder being disregarded.   It is hypothesised that stress

changes the threshold allowing a greater number of signals to be received, but also increasing the false positives.

Using the Selye and the inverted-U models, Weinman (1977) predicted that stress-related disease would occur in exposed employees with a higher risk at both the high and low stress extremes. He examined medical data from 276 senior executives of a financial institution and 1,204 junior executives. Personnel responsibility was the one factor common to both groups. The observed data validated the hypothesis. Specifically, the lower management level group found the major stress in role ambiguity along with work overload, both quantitative and qualitative, while for senior management the stress lay in quantitative overload and conflict.

From a psychological viewpoint Cox and MacKay (1979) emphasise that stress, or by the present definition strain, is a highly individual phenomenon. It exists as a result of a person's appraisal of his involvement in his environment, both physical and psychosocial. Stress (strain) arises as a result of an imbalance between the person's perceptions of the demands made of him, and his perception of his ability to cope.

When stress arises it is associated with a negative emotional experience and with both psychological and physiological change. Job dissatisfaction from the viewpoint of Cox and MacKay may be viewed as part of a cognitive response, and may also be part of the development of alienation from work. The progression of behaviour in response to occupational stress thus may be firstly an immediate reorganisation of the normal profile of behaviour, then the occurrence of activities that can be viewed as abnormal, and finally a disorganisation and disintegration of behaviour, or breakdown.

It has been shown in Chapter 3 that human strain is manifested by physiological and psychological changes mediated via the neuro-endocrine system. Levi and his associates, working on the original demonstration of von Euler and Lundberg (1954), that the physiological activity aroused by emotional stress could in fact be quantified, have gone on to show that there is good evidence for a variety of effects of psychosocial stimuli on neuro-endocrine function (Fröberg and Levi, 1969; Fröberg, Karlsson, Levi, et al., 1970; Kagan and Levi, 1971; Levi, 1964; Levi, 1971; Levi, 1973).

Levi (1970) states: "There is a growing awareness that working life subjects many people to considerable, possibly dangerous, psychosocial stimuli. We commonly speak of the stress of working life, often measuring the consequences of competition, and of the urge for advancement and success. We should, however, not forget that this concept also comprises the consequences of man's exposure to conflict with his fellow workers, to piece-work, disintegration of work processes into isolated routines, shift work, automation, rapid technological change, urbanisation, etc. Technological development has proceeded faster than biological development."

It is argued that any given individual has a certain genetic capacity for adapting to his environment, and has certain forms of coping behaviour for dealing with his environment (Kagan and Levi, 1971). These factors will determine his response to the stress induced by some combination of psychosocial or psychophysical (noise, heat, etc.) stressors, and will determine to a greater or less degree the resulting neuro-endocrine mediated "strain". This "strain" may be manifest as hyper-, hypo- or dysfunction of the cardiovascular, gastro-intestinal, genito-urinary, respiratory, skeletal or other systems, dependent again on genetic and acquired factors, and may be regarded as a precursor of disease. Whether or not actual clinically proven disease does in fact develop by way of this mechanism is still a matter of question. As Levi (1974) remarks: " ... studies demonstrate the probable importance of non-specific psychosocial environmental stimuli and non-specific physiological mechanisms in a variety of diseases. We further conclude that the causation of disease by such stimuli is not proven but that there is a high level of suspicion".

That foregoing statement, of course, was made with respect to stress occurring under very widely varying conditions, many of which had no direct, or even indirect, connection with work stress, some occurring experimentally with human or animal subjects, or some within man-made or natural environments.

Various experiments, however, and controlled observations in the laboratory and in the workplace, have demonstrated that the same type of stress can occur in the daily working environment, with the same type of response, and perhaps with the same potential for clinically manifest disease. Fröberg, Karlsson, Levi et al. (1970) report a series of controlled experiments, some of which simulated extreme conditions while others represented fairly common types of working environment.

Two of these involved military activities, in one of which an older group of officers alternated military staff work with a shooting exercise continuously for a period of 75 hours; in the other a younger group of officers conducted a continuous shooting exercise for 75 hours. In both groups measurable physiological and bio-chemical changes were found, including in the second group evidence of grossly increased neuro-endocrine activity, and reversible changes in the ST-segment and T-wave of the electrocardiogram.

In an experiment more closely related to the environment of commercial enterprise a group of invoice clerks, normally working on salary, were placed over four consecutive days on a payment régime that alternated between salary only and a piece-work bonus. During piece-work the output went up 114 per cent. The subjects, however, complained of mental and physical discomfort, backache, and pain in the shoulders and arms. Catecholamines, i.e. adrenal medullary hormones, increased by 25-40 per cent, a clear index of stress.

In another experimental situation, advantage was taken of the fact that a group of office workers was going to be moved to another building. Some workers who previously operated from small office rooms were moved to "landscaped" open office settings and some retained small offices. It was possible therefore to obtain data pertaining to the act of moving and also to the effect of moving to an open versus a closed office environment. It was observed that in those who moved from a small office to a land-scaped office the effect was such as to raise the catecholamine level for a period of one week before it returned to normal. For those who retained a private office there was an initial rise in catecholamine levels which returned towards the initial level in two days. Effects of fatigue and performance ratings paralleled the catecholamine levels in both cases.

Fröberg and Levi (1969) outline another experiment more closely resembling elements of assembly line work, namely sorting steel balls. Thirty-three volunteer male subjects were divided into three matched groups. One group acted as control and was permitted to sit calmly and comfortably through three two-hour periods. The other groups undertook a sorting task during the middle period to the accompaniment of distracting criticism, noise and lights.   The results in the latter groups showed significantly increases in heart rate, systolic blood pressure and catecholamines.

Various other studies have also been carried out on diverse groups, including supermarket checkout cashiers, paper mill workers, proof-readers, public speakers with speech defects, and audiences watching emotionally arousing films.   All groups have demonstrated essentially the same reactions.   (Levi, 1972.)   Similarity of the reaction in different ethnic groups was also demonstrated by Lazarus et al. (1970) who found the same type of reaction in Japanese and in American subjects watching emotionally disturbing films.

Now, it can be argued that even the longest experiment of 75 hours does not represent normal working conditions, nor does it demonstrate any disease process.   This is true.   The experiments, however, do demonstrate a consistent response with significant physiological and biochemical changes.   It is considered that if these changes are maintained for a sufficiently long period, or repeated sufficiently often, they will in fact give rise to manifest disease.   The required duration or frequency of exposure is not known.   These factors are probably unique to the individual and grossly influenced by a variety of intrinsic and extrinsic interactive factors, so that it becomes difficult if not impossible to predict other than statistically the level at which a psychosocial stress will become hazardous.

From a holistic viewpoint, of course, work stress should not be considered in isolation from the stress of ordinary living.   The work of Holmes and Rahe (1967) and Rahe et al. (1967), and subsequent studies by these workers in what has come to be called life event research, has clearly pointed to a link between the social environment in which people live and their health.   Life event research involves longitudinal studies of individual members of population cohorts, in which they chart the frequency of occurrence of variously rated stressful events over a period of their lives. Using sophisticated interpretation and statistical analysis, an investigator correlates the occurrence of events with the individual's well-being and health.   In this approach, of course, elements of work stress can become life events and contribute to the over-all stress exposure.   There are clearly problems of

selection, reporting, interpretation and rating in this approach
(Cleary, 1974), but the technique has the advantage of placing
work stress in a rational perspective. Lehmann (1975) has
recently recounted the results of a 15-year study of ageing, in
which it was concluded that work satisfaction is the single best
predictor of a long life. He noted that there is evidence that
occupational stress plays an important role in the development of
75 per cent of heart disease.

The presence of alleviating factors in the psychosocial
environment can act to moderate the effect of a particular stressor
or group of stressors. These "mediating variables" have been
examined by a number of researchers. Cobb (1976), for example,
has shown evidence to suggest that in a crisis, which is clearly a
stressful situation, social support can protect persons from a wide
variety of pathological conditions.

Beehr et al. (1976), in fact, have specifically examined the
possibility that such mediators as group cohesiveness, supervisory
support and autonomy can moderate the relationship between the
commonly occurring stressor of role ambiguity and other manifestations of possible strain, namely job dissatisfaction, life dissatisfaction, low self-esteem and depression. It was found, in
particular, that autonomy could alleviate the stress of role
ambiguity. In poorly cohesive groups the relationship between
role ambiguity and low self-esteem was greater than among cohesive
groups, while in cohesive groups there was a stronger relationship
between role ambiguity and job dissatisfaction, a finding that
tends to suggest that job dissatisfaction might be perpetuated in
cohesive groups.

More pragmatic approaches towards delineation of work stress
have been made by other researchers who have looked at the problems
of the worker in his working environment and attempted to relate
them to subsequent stress-induced disease. Since a significant
majority of workers express satisfaction with their work it is
often difficult to demonstrate a direct causal relationship between
work stress and stress-induced disease. Taylor (1974), in a
popular review of the subject, quotes a study from the Federal
Republic of Germany in which 6,000 workers expressed varying degrees
of satisfaction in their work. Nevertheless, one-third of those
questioned complained about the fast rhythm of work, 36 per cent
about the hectic atmosphere, and 42 per cent about nervous strain,

each of these being conditions likely to stimulate excessive neuro-
endocrine response.   He also quotes a study by Dr. P. Raffle of
London Transport, showing a marked increase (over 360 per cent for
sprains, strains, "nerves", debility and headache) in the amount
of sickness absence in 1971-72 as compared with 1953-54.   Since
an actual objective improvement in health could be shown, he
suggested that the increasing levels of absence were of a psychosocial origin.

In a somewhat more experimental approach, Margolis et al.
(1974) defined ten indices of psychosocial strain (over-all physical
health, escapist drinking, depressed mood, self-esteem, life satisfaction, job satisfaction, motivation to wo·k, intention to leave
job, frequency of suggestions to employer, and absenteeism) and six
stressful phenomena (role ambiguity, underutilisation, overload,
resource inadequacy, insecurity, non-participation) and found a
significant correlation with all except one of the indicators, namely
the frequency of suggestions to the employer.   In particular, they
observed that increased stress was associated with poorer "physical
or mental health".

In a comprehensive study among telegraphists, as well as
clerical and technical staff in some major cities in Australia,
Ferguson (1973) related the occurrence of medically identified
absences for "neurotic illnesses" to the work environment of the
absentee workers.   He found the incidence of absence to be higher
among the telegraphists than the clerical workers, and among the
clerical workers than the technicians.   By interview and questionnaire he demonstrated, in comparison with a control group, a negative
attitude to the work, to supervision and to job security among the
identified groups of absentees.   The primary factors comprising the
over-all stressful environment of the telegraphists were identified
as being monotony induced by a job design which permitted long
periods of underloading interspersed with hectic periods of over-
loading, the requirement for a complex of high-level aptitudes,
namely linguistic (coding and decoding), selective vigilance,
decision making, and neuromuscular skills, along with a high level of
agitation and anxiety arising from the ever-present possibility of
making errors.

In another occupational study, this time among air traffic
controllers at Frankfurt Airport, an occupation known to be stressful, Singer and Rutenfranz (1971) observed the same type of pattern.

They noted, however, that while in terms of relative importance of job factors the top five were type of work, pay, job security, opportunity for advancement and conditions of work, the top five in terms of satisfaction were pay, working hours, working conditions, behaviour of supervisors, behaviour of co-workers. In fact, few of the factors that were deemed important actually gave rise to satisfaction although in fact more than 85 per cent of the workers considered themselves satisfied with their work.

There is perhaps a sex-related difference in response, as reported by another Singer (1975), in a later study. He examined stress-related responses in some 1,300 government employees, of whom 153 were female. The stressors included the self-defined difference between personal desires and opportunities for five job characteristics, namely role definition, responsibility for people, workload, utilisation of abilities, and participation, as well as a variety of life stressful events. Results indicated that for males, underutilisation of abilities and lack of participation accounted for more of the variance than did life stressors, while for females the opposite was the case.

The foregoing are illustrative of the type of operationally oriented work that has taken place, but of course various other studies have also been made, including a briefly reported study in Poland by Slawina and Moykin (1975), in which correlations were obtained between work stress and resulting physiological and psychological work strain in over 88,000 people from 525 professions. Strain was defined in terms of "heaviness" or physiological workload, and "tensity" or psychosocial workload, the latter of course including physiological and biochemical components.

Perhaps less comprehensive in terms of numbers of subjects, but reported in fine detail, is the work of Caplan et al. (1975) in the United States, who studied in depth over 2,000 respondents in 23 occupations, to determine whether (a) subjective job stresses (including job demands and poor person-environment fit) would produce strain in the individual exposed; (b) whether individual personality variables would influence that strain; (c) whether higher rate of reported illness is correlated with greater strain; and (d) whether a poor fit between the desired job environment and the perceived job environment will produce stronger effects on strain than either of these environmental states alone. Not all of the vast array of results are significant to this particular

discussion but, inter alia, they observed that the subjective
stress environment is more important as a prediction of strain
than the objective environment, and that subjective reactions such
as anxiety, irritation, depression and somatic complaints are
related to one another and appear to be influenced by dissatisfaction with the work rather than by the actual characteristics of the
work itself. These reactions were highest among machine tenders
and assemblers and lowest in physicians and continuous flow workers.

Physiological measures were obtained on a subsample of 390 subjects (administrators, scientists, supervisors, air traffic controllers, machine-paced assembly-line workers, and electronic
technicians at air traffic control towers). Measures included
pulse rate, systolic and diastolic blood pressure, cortisol, choles-
terol, thyroid hormones and serum uric acid. Contrary to findings in other studies, no first-order correlation was observed
between work stress and the physiological findings. This result
was attributed to two factors: firstly, other previous research
done by the group suggested that a work stress/strain relationship
is normally demonstrable only when some other social or psychological factor or factors is also involved, and secondly such
relationships may perhaps be found only in certain personality
types (e.g. the so-called type A personality - hard driving,
involved in work activities, competitive, time conscious and
achievement oriented).

On the other hand, several findings provided support for the
hypothesis that strain will in turn lead to clinical manifestations,
notably an increase in blood pressure (lowest in the scientists, who
were exposed to the least identified stress), and cardiovascular
disease (coronary disease, arteriosclerosis, circulatory problems,
etc.), where the incidence was found to be highest among the tool
and die makers, machine-paced assemblers, administrative professors,
and accountants, all of whom were rated at high levels of psychosocial stress. It is emphasised, however, that the number of
persons reporting illness was relatively small, and the conclusions
are not definitive.

In general, and in contrast to the popular viewpoint, the
highest levels of stress and resulting strain were found not among
the executives and high-level decision makers but among the
assemblers and relief workers on machine-paced assembly lines.
This finding has been confirmed in another context by Hinkle of the

Bell Telephone Company (cited in Taylor, 1974) who showed that
rates for "heart attack" and coronary death rates for those in the
third decade were 30 per cent less for the university educated
individual than for the individual who had not attended university,
and that those who had not been to college were more susceptible
to high blood pressure and arteriosclerosis.   Those exposed to
greatest stress were foremen and supervisors.

    The relationship of work stress to gastro-intestinal disorders
demands some consideration.   It is not a simple one.   Classical
experiments of Pavlov and Cannon with dogs, as well as Wolf and
Wolf with human gastric fistulae, have demonstrated beyond doubt
the psychic influences on gastric secretion.   It is also clinically
recognised that the patient with gastro-intestinal distress, peptic
ulcer, and intestinal hyper- or hypo-function tends to be anxious
and stressed.   An actual causal relationship, however, can only be
suspected, not directly proven.   Aanonsen (1959) has observed a
higher incidence of peptic ulcer in shift workers and night
workers, particularly where there is frequent change from one
shift to another.   And while this is undoubtedly a form of work
stress, it is one that involves changes in circadian rhythm, as
well as drastic changes in social and nutritional habits.

    Circadian rhythm of course is the term given to the diurnally
cyclic patterns of physiological and biochemical activity and
psychological behaviour inherent in biological function.   Specifically, physiological and biochemical functions such as, for
example, heart rate and sodium excretion, are patterned on a
24-hour cycle, being least between 2-4 a.m. and greatest around
4 p.m.   Similarly, psychological arousal is normally greatest
during daylight hours.   The cycles are entrained by time patterns,
e.g. perceived hour of the day, daylight, eating, working and
social habits.   Disturbance of the pattern, for example by an
artifically lengthened or shortened day, or by a change in
behaviour pattern caused by a change in work shift, will in the
first situation disrupt the entrainment and allow various cyclic
functions to run free, or in the second case will call for
heightened activity when the diurnal cycles are out of phase with
requirements.   In either case, a demonstrable strain may be
generated, manifest by discomfort, reduced arousal and reduced
performance.   Partial adaptation can occur within a few days but
complete adaptation can only occur when all time references are

synchronised.   The more frequently changes in shift occur, particularly if they occur in less than or close to the adaptation
period, the greater the resulting strain.

The situation, however, is further complicated by the motivation of the worker.   Where the shift work, overtime or night work
is desired, the perceived stress is minimised, as is the resulting
strain.   This viewpoint is confirmed by a British National
Economic Development Council Report quoted by Robert Taylor (1974)
which reported that while shift work in the motor vehicle industry
did give rise to social and psychological problems, the workers
were prepared to accept the problems in the light of the associated rewards.   Peter Taylor (1974) at the TUC Centenary Institute
of Occupational Health, in a study of 965 men from 29 plants,
showed also that cardiovascular problems were more common amongst
day workers than amongst night workers and that the latter had less
sickness absence.   This finding, however, could be attributable to
self-selection of the group forming the sample of night workers.

Several conclusions emerge from the foregoing discussion
which can be summarised by stating that from the findings of controlled laboratory experiments, field observations and large-
scale epidemiological investigations, there is a strong evidence
suggesting, although perhaps not proving, a causal relationship
between work stress and resulting dissatisfaction, psychosomatic
disorder and disease.   The relationship is far from simple.   It
involves genetic tendencies and personality factors in the individual, as well as significant stress in the physical and psychosocial environment.   Furthermore, work stress cannot properly be
isolated from life stress, nor is it reasonable to isolate job
satisfaction from life satisfaction.

STRESS AND SATISFACTION: THE INTER-RELATIONSHIP

7

It has been shown that man has to contend both with a physical component of his working environment and a psychosocial component; that conditions in either or both may be unacceptably stressful, and that work, whether physical or skilled, may itself constitute an unacceptable stress. One must also recognise that, in the terms defined, stress is always present to a greater or lesser degree and that paradoxically the total absence of apparent stress becomes in itself a stress. Thus, on the one hand, stress can be considered as a load, increasing to an overload, arising from addition to the man-machine-environment complex of qualities which are undesirable from the human point of view, such as intolerable working conditions, harsh supervision or unreasonable working hours. On the other hand, removal of desirable attributes by, for example, the creation of a stultifying environment, with reduced stimulation and inherently boring work, can act as a kind of negative loading which can be equally stressful. The stress experienced by an individual lies somewhere on the continuum between that arising from removal of desirable qualities and that arising from the addition of undesirable qualities. Thus there is some point where his stress level can be optimum.

In looking at the effects of that stress on an individual's perception of his reaction to his work, one cannot however think only in terms of satisfaction. Accentuation of the positive is a theme beloved of motivational psychologists, and may be politically and administratively desirable, but in examining a stress/strain relationship of this type one must recognise that there comes a time when strain is equated not merely with reduction in satisfaction, but also in generation of dissatisfaction. Thus

satisfaction has to be considered as one end of a satisfaction/
dissatisfaction continuum, where one state merges into the other
through a region of indifference.

It will be observed further that the same elements which are
identified as generators of unacceptable stress are also defined
as dissatisfiers or causes of dissatisfaction. Thus in a stress/
strain analysis, dissatisfaction is a manifestation of strain,
and, correspondingly, satisfaction is a manifestation of a well
adapted response to a level of stress that tends towards the
optimum.

Satisfaction, however, is not an absolute. There is no
upper bound of absolute satisfaction, while the lower bound merges
indistinguishably into dissatisfaction, which itself has no
absolute lower bound. Each is a relative term, relative to some
previous state, or to the state of some other individual.
Furthermore, the pursuit of satisfaction, like the pursuit of
happiness, is seldom a consciously articulated human goal. One
does not normally seek a state of satisfaction. One may seek
various objectives, which one has to a great or lesser extent
defined, and in so doing one may find satisfaction, but normally
one is more concerned with minimising dissatisfaction than maximi-
sing satisfaction. It is a quality, again like happiness, that
tends to be seen more in retrospect than in prospect.

Not only, then, is job satisfaction part of an unbounded
continuum, it is also a personal state, as opposed to a group state,
and its goals will vary from person to person, from circumstance to
circumstance and from time to time in the same person. Furthermore, it is at least as much a function of the individual as of the
job, with connotations of positive well-being which are barely
consistent with reality and probably attainable at best by only a
few. The majority of people, the majority of the time, are
neither particularly satisfied nor particularly dissatisfied. They
occupy some shifting range in between, satisfied about some things,
dissatisfied about others, dynamically adjusting to each change in
their individual homeostatic equilibria. Thus, data pertaining to
the level of job satisfaction of groups have to be interpreted with
caution. At best they are statistical indices which have often
little or no application to the individual.

Not only do the data have to be interpreted with caution, but the adoption and implementation of measures to promote job satisfaction on the basis of these data should be predicated on the realisation that the expected results may not materialise.

It is true that one can broadly define certain attributes of job satisfaction, such as those discussed in earlier chapters, and for that matter one can define even more easily certain attributes of dissatisfaction. It would probably be naive, however, to consider that if the defined dissatisfiers were minimised and the satisfiers were maximised then a state of job satisfaction would persist. This indeed is one of the goals of work humanisation programmes, and a worthy goal it is, even if its only effect were to be a general raising of the quality of working life. But it should not be assumed that work humanisation per se will lead to persisting job satisfaction. The goals of work satisfaction are ephemeral and recede as they are approached. As has been discussed in earlier chapters, the human capacity to adapt is such that were these goals ever achieved man would adapt to the new level of living, accept it as a norm, and seek still further levels of satisfaction. The nature of human physiology and psychology, as illustrated by the Hawthorne experiments and numerous other studies of many related and unrelated varieties in field and laboratory, determines that, given an environment, or a machine-environment system, where his homeostasis is not threatened, man responds favourably to change in state, not to achievement of a static state, provided that the combination of magnitude and rate of change is not too great. The change is preferably, but not even necessarily, towards a more favoured state. Where the combination of magnitude and rate of change is within acceptable limits, as perceived by the individual, then his arousal, alertness, interest, performance capability and indeed satisfaction are maintained at a high level. Where the environment threatens his homeostasis, where the magnitude and/or rate of change are too great, or not great enough (which also threatens his homeostasis), then there will be stress, expressed at least initially as dissatisfaction.

Bearing these factors in mind, and oversimplifying for the sake of clarity, it will be seen that the basic relationship between human stress and job satisfaction can be represented by a classic bell-shaped curve. The greatest satisfaction is found

where the stress level is optimum.   As you remove desirable
features or add undesirable features the level of satisfaction
drops through a zone of indifference until finally it becomes dissatisfaction.   It is emphasised however that the curve is a
schematic curve, and while no doubt it will always retain a bell
shape it will not necessarily retain the same proportions;
indeed there is little doubt that the shape will be in a state of
continuous change, reflecting the continuous adjustment of the
system as it responds to disturbances in equilibrium.

SOME REMEDIAL SUGGESTIONS

8

In a study such as this, where the facts are insubstantial and
many of the considerations are drawn on the basis of inference, it
is not difficult to make a list of areas where knowledge is lacking,
since it is inadequate in all areas.   Consequently no such list
will be presented.   Instead, an attempt will be made to highlight
areas which appear to be of particular significance.

Again, however, while it is possible to outline areas where
some particular viewpoint should be emphasised or some action taken,
it is not so easy in many cases to say exactly how such a remedial
suggestion should be implemented.   The suggestions presented
below, however, are believed to be of significance.   Some refer
to suggested courses of action, some to the need for support in
various areas of research, and some to the desirability of adoption
of a particular point of view.   The fact that suggestions have not
been made in certain areas should not be construed as meaning that
these areas are not important.   There are no suggestions, for
example, pertaining to the study of stress-related diseases or life
event research, because considerable investigation is already
taking place in these vitally important areas.

Desired relationship - ergonomics and work humanisation

The key to the solution of job satisfaction problems may well
lie in the combination of ergonomics concepts with making work more
human programmes.   It would seem that making work more human to
date has been approached on a somewhat empirical basis.   Various
groups or companies have decided, largely on the basis of personal
experience, aided by wise advice, that certain radically different

forms of management procedure, or practice, might be beneficial in improving working morale, and, hopefully, production. Sometimes these have been effective and sometimes not.

The possible role of ergonomics in guiding and orienting some of these activities, however, has not yet been discussed to any extent (Fraser, 1978). Ergonomics is defined as the study of the anatomical, physiological and psychological aspects of man in his working environment, with a view to the ultimate optimisation of safety, health, comfort and efficiency. As a broadly based, operationally oriented, transdisciplinary subject, it includes amongst its activities various concerns such as work study, design for human use, human factors, human engineering, and environmental management, each of which can be appropriately defined. In some eastern European countries, indeed, ergonomics also includes some subjects more commonly considered elsewhere under the headings of occupational health and hygiene. While indeed it is fairly easy to define the difference in the approach and activities of ergonomists and those engaged in occupational health and hygiene, it is not very meaningful at this time since there is an undoubted overlap, just as there is, for example, between the work of architects and planners.

The major role of ergonomics in relation to making work more human, however, most probably lies in its application to the analysis and design of existing and planned systems, with a view to optimising the function of the human component of the system. Little, if anything, however, has yet been done to examine the role and relationships of ergonomics to job satisfaction per se, although much work has been done that demonstrates its effectiveness in given situations. The International Symposium in Bucharest, Romania, on Practical Applications of Ergonomics in Industry, Agriculture and Forestry (ILO, 1974) presented numerous examples to this end, while at an earlier symposium, Lambert (1969) outlined some of the more general relationships.

In a given situation the approach might include the following sequence of events:

(a) analysis of the existing system including the extent of human participation;
(b) generation of design alternatives;

(c) development of design selection criteria to allow for optimi-
     sation of safety, health, comfort and efficiency, and to pro-
     mote opportunity for satisfaction of higher order needs
     appropriate to the work;
(d) development of measurement techniques to validate the solution
     or solutions chosen;
(e) implementation of the chosen solution; and
(f) validation of the new or redesigned system.

     Clearly the foregoing is a broad overview that requires much
amplification.   It is therefore suggested that a study be undertaken to determine the role of ergonomics in the implementation of
making work more human and the promotion of job satisfaction.

Job satisfaction as an issue

     It has been noted earlier that the evidence derived from
attitude surveys seems to suggest that job satisfaction per se is
not in fact an issue amongst the majority of workers, although the
evidence on which to base any conclusion is in fact very inadequate.
It was suggested that the workforce as a group tends to be inarticulate on the subject of job satisfaction since it is not indeed an
objective for which one normally strives, and that while workers do
not in general consider themselves particularly satisfied or dissatisfied, the majority do indeed appear to present a shifting dissatisfaction from time to time and circumstance to circumstance.
However, while observers of the work scene support this point of
view, more concrete evidence is needed to determine to what extent
the large non-committed majority are in fact dissatisfied; how and
when, if at all, does that dissatisfaction shift; what are the
factors involved in influencing any shift; to what extent do those
who claim satisfaction or dissatisfaction actually maintain their
commitment, etc.   This information can best be obtained by longitudinal field study.   It is therefore suggested that studies be
encouraged in these areas.

Measurement of job satisfaction

     As has been discussed, job satisfaction or dissatisfaction is
an index of the level of stress perceived by the worker.   Unfortunately, there is no adequate scale for the measurement of job satisfaction.   As noted before, a given level of job satisfaction

describes a position on a satisfaction/dissatisfaction continuum, and reflects attitudes not only with regard to the job but also with respect to the individual's perception of his entire social and other ambiance.

Furthermore, one might question in some instances the selection of independent variables employed in some of the studies relating job satisfaction or dissatisfaction to some evidence of stress. In this regard absenteeism and labour turnover are not infrequently used as an indication of disaffection. Verhaegen (1979) notes that while absenteeism and turnover each have something to do with satisfaction or dissatisfaction they are influenced by so many other factors that only in some concrete situation can differences in absenteeism be related in an unequivocal way to differences in satisfaction. He goes on to suggest that progress in this field will depend on longitudinal studies, in which people are questioned on their concrete, changing, job-connected values, and the aspects of their work to which they attribute their satisfaction or dissatisfaction, and that work tasks must be correlated with changes in satisfaction, not over six months but over years, in order to exclude short-lived Hawthorne effects.

At this time, carefully interpreted individual attitude surveys, backed up by individual interviews in depth, probably provide the best index of job satisfaction, but they have considerable limitations in implementation and interpretation which have been discussed earlier. There is much need for some validated index or indices of job satisfaction based on large-scale cross-correlation of work attitude surveys with other measures of social behaviour, such as those discussed and referenced by Christian (1974) in his presentation to the Organisation for Economic Co-operation and Development. The approach that might be involved would include both direct attitudinal surveys and interviews, as well as direct observation of behaviour in the work environment and in society at large, with the object of compiling indices of work-related behaviour and indices of social behaviour, with subsequent correlation. Until some large-scale longitudinal study is undertaken and an attempt made to present job satisfaction in at least semi-quantitative terms, the compilation and interpretation of comparative studies is grossly limited.

It is therefore suggested that the work currently being done in the general area of social indices be expanded to include specific studies to determine the relationship between job satisfaction and life satisfaction with a view to developing indices or measures of job satisfaction.

Social and biological influences on job satisfaction

The various social and biological factors such as ethnic background, cultural habit patterns, either local or general, age and sex may have an influence on one's perception of job satisfaction, but in fact there is very little information on the nature and extent of that influence. One might speculate, or hypothesise, for example, on the significance of the puritan work ethic on attitudes to job satisfaction, or sex differences in its perception, but in fact little is actually known in these areas. It is therefore suggested that research be encouraged to determine to what extent, if any, there are consistent cultural, ethnic, sex and age differences in the perception of work satisfaction/dissatisfaction, and how these differences, if indeed they are demonstrable, might affect, for example, making work humanisation programmes or other measures designed to improve job satisfaction.

Studies on the effect of change

Interest, arousal and alertness seem to be more readily maintained in the presence of change. It would be desirable to determine to what extent planned environmental, procedural and other forms of operationally oriented change are feasible in industry, to modify human behaviour, and to what extent such change is beneficial and related to job satisfaction. Studies should be undertaken in laboratory controlled conditions to confirm the effect of change and to determine the relationships that exist among such factors as the type of change effected, the magnitude of change, the frequency and rate of change, etc., with a view to defining optimum strategies. These should then be validated in field studies. It is therefore suggested that support be given to this type of research on both a short-term and a long-term basis.

Making work more human and job satisfaction

Programmes for making work more human constitute one of the most significant recent advances in the improvement of human condi-

tions in industry.   In the light of the human desire for change
and continued stimulus in the working environment, it is worth while
to re-examine in part the fundamental nature of the concept of its
implementation.

It was shown earlier that, within limits, man will adapt to any
reasonable environment into which he is placed, and will continue
to adapt as the environment changes within circumscribed limits.
He is dissatisfied as the environment becomes static.   In fact one
of the indices of his maturity is his capacity to endure an
increasingly static environment.   A totally static environment is,
however, a severe stress.   Making work more human is a goal-
oriented concept which looks towards the achievement of some ultimate
ideal.   The end then is effectively a static state.   So long as
the process of achieving humanisation is in action, the individual
will react, no doubt favourably.   When the process ceases there is
nothing more to react to.   Perhaps then, instead of considering
making work more human to be goal-oriented, it should be considered
process-oriented.   It is therefore suggested that while the ultimate goal of a higher quality of life should remain the ideal,
emphasis should be placed more on the process of its achievement
than on the nature of the actual goal, more on the change than on
the attainment.   In this manner, as designers and marketers of
consumer goods have clearly established, interest is maintained at
a higher level and the potential for new satisfaction is continually
available.

In other words, while continuing to seek to make work more
human and a higher quality of life, greater emphasis in policy and
programmes should be placed on controlled change within the environment, in work procedures, and in work content, under various limits
yet to be defined, even if the actual quality of work conditions
advances more slowly.

Systems approach to human studies

The final suggestion is perhaps even more complex and
intangible, since it concerns the attitudes and viewpoints of those
who deal with the very areas that have been under discussion, such
as stress, industrial health and hygiene, conditions of work and
job satisfaction.   There are still planners and others in these
areas who have not yet realised the unity of a man-machine-
environment system.   This recommendation is essentially a plea to

recognise that even when one is working with empirically labelled entities such as job satisfaction, or conditions of work, or social relationships, one is in fact dealing with an interactive system. It may be procedurally necessary to isolate components or sub-components of that system for various purposes, but one must always recognise that in modifying a component the entire system is ultimately affected in sometimes unpredictable ways.

In certain quarters, the term "systems approach" has almost become a cliché, but cliché notwithstanding, a systems approach to human studies serves to create the structure in which human problems can be examined in their entirety.

It is therefore suggested that institutions and individuals alike consciously recognise and emphasise in their planning, their practice, and their policies that man in his working environment is an integral and interactive part of a man-machine-environment system, and that while for practical purposes components of that system may require individual consideration, no part of that system functions in isolation, and any modification affecting one part will ultimately affect the whole.

It has been shown, then, that a complex interaction does indeed occur involving human stress, work and satisfaction; that work stress is part of the stress of living, and that satisfaction in work is in part an expression of satisfaction in life. It is the total effect that is manifest in man, not merely the effect of work. In today's industrial society, however, dissatisfaction for many seems to be at least as common as satisfaction, although no one state perhaps remains dominant. The severity of the stress so induced can approach or surpass the tolerance level and be associated with disturbance and disability.

As the writer and humanist, Paul Gascar, has remarked (1968): "Besides, our way of life today, the strain of modern civilisation, has created a new range of health problems derived from stress. Nervous exhaustion, noise, the pressure of the crowd, the assault of propaganda and advertising, the obliteration of the individual personality - these and similar factors have contributed to a steady rise in the incidence of illnesses of nervous origin. Such ill-nesses cannot be identified or treated by conventional methods."

Perhaps, however, and despite its positive connotations, emphasis on the attainment of satisfaction on the job, at work, or even in life is not one of the most fruitful objectives. Achievement of satisfaction does not seem to be a human goal. Perhaps, indeed, effort should be concentrated more on reducing stress in the workplace, and if possible in daily living, to levels that are compensable by the normal physiological and psychological processes, thereby reducing human strain, minimising dissatisfaction, and hopefully lessening the likelihood of psychosomatic disorder.

REFERENCES

A. Aanonsen: "Medical problems of shift work", in Industrial Medicine and Surgery, 1959, No. 28, pp. 422-427.

C.R. Anderson: "Coping behaviours as intervening mechanisms in the inverted-U stress-performance relationship", in Journal of Applied Psychology, 1976, No. 61, pp. 30-34.

M. Argyle: The social psychology of work (Harmondsworth, Mddx., Penguin Books, 1972).

J. Barbash: Job satisfaction and attitude surveys (Organisation for Economic Co-operation and Development, Document OECD-MS/IR/ 74.31, Paris, 1974).

J. Barbash: "Humanizing work - a new ideology", in AFL-CIO American Federationist (Washington, DC), July 1977 (abstract).

F.C. Bartlett: "Fatigue following highly skilled work", in Proceedings of the Royal Society, Series B, 1943, No. 131, pp. 247-257.

F.C. Bartlett: "Psychological criteria of fatigue", in W.F. Floyd and A.T. Welford (eds.): Symposium on Fatigue (London, H.C. Lewis, 1953).

T.A. Beehr, J.R. Walsh and T.D. Taber: "Relationship of stress to individually or organizationally valued states: Higher order needs as a moderator", in Journal of Applied Psychology, 1966, No. 61, pp. 41-47.

A. Berthoz: L'ergonomie: Peut-elle réellement permettre d'améliorer les conditions de travail? (1975).

C. Cameron: "A theory of fatigue", in Ergonomics, No. 16, 1973, pp. 633-648.

R.D. Caplan, S. Cobb, J.R.P. French (Jr.), R.V. Harrison, S.R. Pruneau: Job demands and worker health: Main effects and occupational differences, US Department of Health Education and Welfare, Public Service Centre for Disease Control, National Institute for Occupational Safety and Health. Research Report (NIOSH), 1975, pp. 75-160

G. Carlestam, L. Levi: Urban conglomerates as psychosocial human stressors, Report to the United Nations Conference on the Human Environment (Royal Ministry of Foreign Affairs, Royal Ministry of Agriculture, Sweden, 1971).

J. Carpentier: "Organisational techniques and the humanisation of work", in International Labour Review (Geneva, ILO), Aug. 1974, pp. 93-116.

CECA: Les facteurs humains et la sécurité. Etudes de physiologie et de psychologie du travail No. 1 (1967).

S. Cobb: "Social support as a moderator of life stress", in Psychosomatic Medicine, 1976, No. 38, pp. 300-314.

T. Cox, C.J. MacKay: "The impact of repetitive work", in R.G. Sell and P. Shipley (eds.): Satisfactions in work design (London, Taylor and Francis, 1979).

D.E. Christian: Social indicators. The OECD experience, presented to the Organisation for Economic Co-operation and Development (Paris, June 1974).

P.J. Cleary: Life events and disease. A review of the methodology and findings (Laboratory for Clinical Stress Research, Karolinska Sjukhuset), 1974, Rept. No. 37.

J.M. Clerc: "Experiments in humanising the organisation of industrial work: Some points from a symposium", in Bulletin (Geneva, International Institute for Labour Studies), 1973, No. 11.

D.R. Davis: "The disorganisation of behaviour in fatigue", in Journal of Neurology and Psychology, 1946, No. 9, pp. 23-29.

Y. Delamotte, K.F. Walker: "Humanisation of work and the quality of working life: Trends and issues", in Bulletin (Geneva, International Institute for Labour Studies), 1973, No. 11.

B.K. Doane, W. Mahatoo, W. Heron, T.H. Scott: "Changes in perceptual function after isolation", in Canadian Journal of Psychology, 1959, No. 13, p. 210.

G.C. Drew: An experimental study of mental fatigue. Air Ministry Flying Personnel Research Committee Report No. 227, Great Britain, 1940.

O.G. Edholm: The biology of work (London, World University Library, 1967).

U.S. Van Euler, U. Lundberg: "Effect of flying on the epinephrin excretion in Air Force personnel", in Journal of Applied Physiology, 1954, No. 6, p. 551.

FAO: Dietary Survey. Their techniques and interpretation, Nutritional Studies No. 4 (Washington, DC, 1949).

D. Ferguson: "A study of occupational stress and health", in Ergonomics, 1973, No. 16, pp. 649-664.

G.A. Fox: Personnel selection, vocational guidance and job satisfaction, Proceedings of Seminar on Job Satisfaction (Division of Occupational Health and Pollution Control, Department of Health, NSW, Australia, 1971).

T.M. Fraser: "Job satisfaction and work humanization: An expanding role for ergonomics", in Ergonomics, 1978, No. 21, pp. 11-19.

T.M. Fraser: "System safety in recreational and powered vehicles", in Human Factors, 1974, No. 16, pp. 474-480.

T.M. Fraser, A.H. Schwichtenburg: "The reliability and quality assurance of man in a man-machine system", in Journal of Environmental Science, 1964, No. 7, pp. 18-22.

J. Fröberg, C-G. Karlsson, L. Levi, L. Ledberg, K. Seeman: "Conditions of work. Psychological and endocrine stress reactions", in Archives of Environmental Health, 1970, No. 21, pp. 789-797.

J. Fröberg, L. Levi: Neuroendocrine measures of work-induced stress: Experimental and real-life studies, Paper presented at XVI International Congress on Occupational Health, Tokyo, 1969.

P. Gascar: "Putting technology in its place", in World Health (Geneva, WHO), March 1968, pp. 50-55.

B. von H. Gilmer: "Attitudes, job satisfaction and industrial morale", in Industrial Psychology (New York, McGraw Hill Book Company, 1961), Chap. 10.

J.H. Goldthorpe et al.: The affluent worker: Industrial attitudes and behaviour (Cambridge, The University Press, 1963).

E. Grandjean: "Fatigue: Its physiological and psychological significance", in Ergonomics, 1968, No. 11, pp. 427-436.

W. Heron: Cognitive and physiological effects of perceptual isolation, Proceedings of Symposium on Sensory Deprivation, Harvard Medical School (Cambridge, Harvard University Press, 1961).

F. Herzberg: Work and the nature of man (New York, World Publishing, 1966).

W.R. Hess: "Stammganglien-Reizversucke", in Berichte über die gesamte Physiologie und experimentelle Pharmakologie, 1927, No. 42, pp. 554-555.

M.J. Hill et al.: Men out of work: A study of unemployment in three English towns (Cambridge, The University Press, 1973).

T.H. Holmes, H. Rahe: "The social readjustment rating scale", in Journal of Psychosomatic Research, 1967, No. 11, pp. 213-218.

J.W. Hunt: Job satisfaction and the organization, Proceedings of Seminar on Job Satisfaction (Division of Occupational Health and Pollution Control, Department of Health, NSW, Australia, 1971).

ILO 1974a. Recent events and developments affecting salaried employees and professional workers, Advisory Committee on Salaried Employees and Professional Workers, 7th Session (Geneva).

- 1974b. Action of the ILO: Problems and perspectives, Report of the Director-General to the International Labour Conference (59th Session, Geneva).

- 1974c. <u>Human values in social policy. An ILO agenda for Europe</u>, Report of the Director-General to the Second European Regional Conference (Geneva).

- 1975a. <u>Making work more human</u>, Report of the Director-General to the International Labour Conference (60th Session, Geneva).

- 1975b. <u>Information note on the ILO and job satisfaction or humanisation of work</u>, Paper submitted to the Conference of European Trade Union Centres on Humanisation of the Working Environment (Geneva).

- 1977. <u>Ergonomics in industry, agriculture and forestry</u>, Occupational Safety and Health Series No. 35 (Geneva).

R. Johnston: "Some characteristics of workers in the building industry", in <u>Journal of Industrial Relations</u>, 1973, No. 15, pp. 105-107.

R. Johnston: "Another union", in <u>Journal of Industrial Relations</u>, 1975, No. 17, pp. 30-43.

R. Johnston, J.C. Cherard: "Workers' attitudes to their jobs", in <u>Economic Activity</u>, Oct. 1970, pp. 37-47.

R.L. Kahn: "The meaning of work: interpretation and proposals for measurement", in Angus, Campbell and Philip E. Couvers (eds.): <u>The human meaning of social change</u> (Russell Sage Foundation, New York, 1972).

A.R. Kagan, L. Levi: <u>Health and environment - psychosocial stimuli. A review</u> (Laboratory for Clinical Stress Research, Karolinska Sjikhuset, Rept. No. 27, 1971).

W.A. Kerr: "Accident proneness of factory departments", in <u>Journal of Applied Psychology</u>, 1950, No. 34, pp. 167-170.

G. Lambert: "Ergonomie et industrialisation", in ILO: <u>Ergonomics and Machine Design</u>, Vol. II, pp. 991-1009, Occupational Safety and Health Series No. 14 (Geneva, 1969).

R.S. Lazarus: <u>Psychological stress and the coping process,</u> (McGraw Hill Book Company, New York, 1967).

R.S. Lazarus, E.M. Opton, J.R. Averill: <u>Cross cultural studies</u>, Proceedings of 1st International Symposium on Society, Stress and Disease (Session 1) (WHO and University of Uppsala, Sweden, 1970).

G. Lehmann: "Physiological measurement as a basis of work organisation in industry", in <u>Ergonomics</u>, 1957, No. 1, pp. 197-203.

P. Lehmann: "Job stress: hidden hazard", in <u>Job Safety and Health</u>, 1975, No. 2, pp. 4-10; abstracted in Excerpta Medica (Occupational Health and Industrial Medicine), Vol. 56, Sect. 35, abstract No. 1998.

L. Levi: "The stress of everyday work as reflected in productiveness, subjective feelings and urinary output of adrenaline and noradrenaline under salaried and piecework conditions", in <u>Journal of Psychosomatic Research</u>, 1964, No. 8, pp. 199-202.

L. Levi: The psycho-social environment and psychosomatic diseases,
   Proceedings of an International Interdisciplinary Symposium
   (WHO and University of Uppsala, Sweden, 1970).

L. Levi: "Stress and distress in response to psycho-social stimuli",
   in Suppl. No. 528, Acta Medica Scandinavia, Vol. 191, 1972.

L. Levi: "Stress, distress and psycho-social stimuli", in Occupational Health, 1973, No. 3, pp. 2-9.

L. Levi, L. Anderson: Population, environment and the quality of
   life, Report to the United Nations World Population Conference
   (Royal Ministry for Foreign Affairs, Sweden, 1974).

T.M. Ling: "Major psycho-social problems of industry", in T.M. Ling
   (ed.): Mental health and human relations in industry (London,
   H.K. Lewis and Co., 1954).

C.B. Little: "Technical-professional unemployment: Middle-class
   adaptability to personal crisis", in The Society Quarterly, 1978,
   No. 17, pp. 262-274.

T.A. Lloyd-Davies: "Society and work", in T.M. Ling (ed.): Mental
   health and human relations in industry (London, H.K. Lewis and
   Co., 1954).

J. Mansell: Dealing with some obstacles to innovation in the work-
   place. Issues in the quality of working life, Occasional paper
   No. 1 (Ontario Ministry of Labour, Quality of Working Life
   Centre, 1980).

B.L. Margolis, W.H. Kroes, R.P. Quinn: "Job stress: an unlisted
   occupational hazard", in Journal of Occupational Medicine, 1974,
   No. 16, pp. 659-661.

A.H. Maslow: Motivation and personality (New York, Harper and
   Row, 1954).

R. McFarland: "Fatigue in industry: Understanding fatigue in
   modern life", in Ergonomics, 1971, No. 14, pp. 1-10.

J.D. Mills: "Job satisfaction in large factories", Personnel
   Practice Bulletin (Department of Labour and National Service,
   Australia), 1967, No. 23, pp. 252-260.

G. Moruzzi, H.W. Magoun: "Brain stem reticular formation and
   activation of the EEG", in Electroencephalography and Clinical
   Neurophysiology, 1949, No. 1, pp. 455-473.

K.F.H. Murrell: Ergonomics. Man in his working environment
   (Chap. 17)(London, Chapman and Hall, 1965).

O. Neuloh, H. Ruke, O. Graf: Der Arbeitsünfall und seine Ursachen
   (Stuttgart, Dusseldorf, Ring Verlag, 1957).

R.H. Rahe, J.D. McKean, R.J. Arthur: "A longitudinal study of life
   change and illness patterns", in Journal of Psychosomatic Research,
   1967, No. 10, pp. 355-366,

F.J. Roethlisberger, W.J. Dickson: Management and the worker
   (Cambridge, Mass., Harvard University Press, 1939).

H. Selye: "The physiology and pathology of exposure to stress", in ACTA Inc. (Montreal, Canada, Medical Publishers, 1950).

H. Selye: "The concept of stress in experimental physiology", in J.M. Tanner (ed.): Stress and psychiatric disorder (Oxford, Blackwell, 1960).

H. Selye: "Stress and aerospace medicine", in Aerospacial Medicine, 1973, No. 44, pp. 190-193.

H. Selye: "Stress without distress", in World Health (Geneva, WHO), Dec. 1974, pp. 3-11.

R. Singer, J. Rutenfranz: "Attitudes of air traffic controllers at Frankfurt Airport", in Ergonomics, 1971, No. 14, pp. 633-639.

J.N. Singer: Job strain as a function of job and life stresses, Ph.D. Dissertation, Colorado State University, 1975.

W.T. Singleton: "Some conceptual and operational doubts about job satisfaction", in R.G. Sell and P. Shipley (eds.): Satisfaction in work design (London, Taylor and Francis, 1979).

S.E. Slawina, Y.V. Moykin: Methods of evaluation of heaviness and tensity of work. Medzynarodowe Sympozyum Naukowe, Poznam, Polska. (Translation), 1975.

J.S. Slotkin: From field to factory (Free Press of Glencoe, Illinois, 1960).

R. Taylor: "Stress at work", in New Society, 1974, No. 30, pp. 139-143.

C. Vamplew: "Automated process operators: Work attitudes and hehaviour", in British Journal of Industrial Relations, 1973, No. 11, pp. 415-439.

P. Verhaegen: "Work satisfaction in present day working life: ergonomics and work satisfaction", in R.E. Sell and P. Shipley (eds.): Satisfaction in work design (London, Taylor and Francis, 1979).

C.R. Walker, R.H. Guest: The man on the assembly line (Cambridge, Mass., Harvard University Press, 1952).

A.T. Welford: "Stress and performance", in Ergonomics, 1973, No. 16, pp. 567-580.

C.G. Weiman: "A study of occupational stressors and the incidence of disease/risk", in Journal of Occupational Medicine, 1977, No. 19, pp. 119-122.

WHO: "Environmental influences on mental health", in Health Hazards of the Human Environment (Geneva, 1972), pp. 152 et seq.

WHO: "The work environment", in Health Hazards of the Human Environment (Geneva, 1972), p. 131.